LEVERAGING THE CORPORATE BRAND

BY

JAMES R. GREGORY

WITH

JACK G. WIECHMANN

NTC Business Books
a division of NTC/Contemporary Publishing Company
Lincolnwood, Illinois USA

Library of Congress Cataloging-in-Publication Data

Gregory, James R.
    Leveraging the corporate brand / by James R. Gregory with Jack G.
Wiechmann.
      p.   cm.
    Includes bibliographical references and index.
    ISBN 0-8442-3444-3 (alk. paper)
    1. Brand name products—Marketing—Management.   I. Wiechmann,
Jack G. II. Title.
HF5415.13.G753   1997
658.8'27--dc21   96-48113
                                                               CIP

Published by NTC Business Books, a division of NTC/Contemporary Publishing Company
4255 West Touhy Avenue
Lincolnwood (Chicago), Illinois 60646-1975, U.S.A.

This book is dedicated to the memory of
Walter Lorenz

A client and friend
who taught me the value of quality,
integrity, and service.

CONTENTS

CHAPTER 10   HOW CORPORATE BRANDING WORKS FOR THE SMALL BUSINESS   129

CHAPTER 11   ADVOCACY AND CAUSE MARKETING   139

CHAPTER 12   INTERACTIVE MEDIA . . . AND STRONG BRAND POSITION   155

FOREWORD

When I first met Jim Gregory, he had just completed his book, *Marketing Corporate Image: The Company As Your Number One Product.* That was in 1992, when expenditures on corporate advertising had just reached their lowest point in recent history. So I asked Jim, "Why in the world would you write a book on this subject at this time?" He answered, "Because Corporate America needs it now more than ever."

And he was right. Through all the reorganizing, restructuring, reengineering, spin-offs, mergers, and acquisitions of recent times, many companies and their brands lost valuable identities—and saw their corporate reputations seriously damaged.

These events established the need for this new book, *Leveraging the Corporate Brand,* as well as for Jim Gregory's other work in helping organizations of all kinds understand, craft, and gauge the value of their own dynamic corporate brands. Most important have been his strides in developing a reliable method to measure the effectiveness of corporate and brand advertising in terms of reputation and financial performance.

Over the years in my dealings with advertisers as vice president of advertising at *The Wall Street Journal* and as publisher of *Barrons,* I've often been asked, "Is there some way I can show my CEO an actual return on our advertising investment?" They were frustrated—and so was I—because although we knew advertising helps build corporate reputation and improve financial performance, there was no way to prove it.

Now we have a book which describes in detail not only the "how-to's" of measuring communications effectiveness, but shows how leading companies such as CIGNA, AT&T, and 3M use integrated communications to reach corporate goals.

You'll learn about the process Jim Gregory has developed which helps companies understand the value of communications and their effect on familiarity, favorability, cash flow, and stock price. His Corporate Branding Index (R) is a proven tool to measure your own company's results and to show how you stack up against the competition.

This book will benefit a broad range of business readers, from corporate CEOs to advertising agency executives, CFOs to investor relations directors, corporate communications executives to vice presidents of marketing, and all others interested in learning how to use corporate branding as the leading edge of corporate strategy.

Bernard T. Flanagan
Vice President, Marketing
Dow Jones & Company, Inc.

ACKNOWLEDGMENTS

Without help, guidance, and encouragement by many individuals, this book would never have come into being. The author is deeply indebted to each and every one of them: advertisers, agency and media executives, and in particular our clients, coworkers, and friends. I am especially grateful to Richard Hagle of NTC Publishing Group for his constant and unfailing attention and support.

Two valuable partners in the process from the corporate side are Richard Costello, GE, and Rupert Smith, GTE, who have remained steadfastly supportive of our efforts to identify the drivers of reputation and to define the value of communications. Without their support and guidance, we would still be looking for that "holy grail."

I wish to offer a special thank you to Jack Frey and Brad Puckey who have been of invaluable help in providing the insight and analysis of the volumes of data that eventually became the basis of the Corporate Branding Index.

I am also deeply indebted to: David A. Aaker Michael Allen, Bill Altermatt, Donald Bainton, L. Wayne Beavers, Bruce Berger, Gail Blanke, Leslie Breland, Charles Brymer, Russell Carson, Kenneth D. Cole, Carol Bruckner Coles, Peter Crawford, Robert A. Crooke, Graham Davis, Ken Dickerson, Edward A. Faruolo, Anne Finucane, Bernard T. Flanagan, Jim Foster, Bradley T. Gale, R. Donald Gamache, Jim Garrity, Richard Garvey, Ralph F. Hake, James R. Harman, Hal Heaslip, Dr. Jeffrey Hudsher, Richard Jackson, R. Steven Johnston, Thomas Keeton, Fred Kremer Jr., Mary Lou Kromer, Robert F. Lauterborn, Robert Lear, Katherine Lee, Theodore Levitt, Larry Light, Ed MacEwen, Alex A. Meyer, James A. Miles, W. Sanford Miller, Mark Misercola, Richard Moe, Philip Mooney, Bruce T. Moorhouse, Bob O'Leary, John Onoda, William Pate, Laura Patterson, Marvin Raber, Joe Renosky, Richard Sabo, Charles G. Salmans, Sanford C. Schulert, Don E. Schultz, Phil Sievers, James D. Speros, Rob Swadosh, Brian Thompson, J. Desmond Towey, Terre Tuzzolino, W. David Vining, Joan H. Walker, Elizabeth Wanger, David R. Whitwam, Daniel Yankelovich.

I must also include in my appreciation the American Association of Advertising Agencies (AAAA), the Association of National Advertisers (ANA), and the American Business Press (ABP). All helped greatly in the collection of valuable data.

Particular recognition belongs to our Corporate Branding Partnership clients whose loyalty, interest, and experience have contributed so much to the completion of this project.

Special thanks go also to the staff of Corporate Branding Partnership who gave so much of their time and support. Most notable is Jack G. Wiechmann who once again put the concepts and words to paper. My gratitude also to Chris Bliss, Maria Candiloro, Denny Davidoff, Jeanine M. DeMarco, Jef Frankum, Michael Glass, Karen Harman, Chris Kauffman, Amy Letteney, Larry McNaughton, Jay Moody, Catherine Ostheimer, Tricia Rattray, Bruno Santini, Doreen Smith.

INTRODUCTION

Not long after the publication of my first book, *Marketing Corporate Image: The Company As Your Number One Product,* I began to realize it was resonating with my readers—perhaps even helping ignite a revolution in corporate communications. The way business people thought about corporate image was changing radically and rapidly. A number of corporate executives, media leaders, and agency executives also perceived the changes and sought our counsel.

They understood that corporate communications was fast becoming essential, if not crucial, to total corporate success. They wanted to know more about the subject: about how its impact on return on investment could be measured and how it might help their companies and clients move profitably into the twenty-first century.

Here indeed was a subject for a second book, with a ready audience of management executives, ranging from the newly minted MBA up to the CEO.

Leveraging the Corporate Brand takes up where *Marketing Corporate Image* leaves off. There is, however, a major difference between the books. Whereas the first book investigated the many facets and uses of corporate image, the present book explores what I call *corporate branding.*

While not an entirely new concept, corporate branding is a new way of marketing for many businesses. It stems, of course, from product branding, which is nothing more than the offer of an explicit or implicit promise to the customer that a particular product—or the company itself—will deliver on its claim and fulfill expectations raised by previous experiences. Corporate branding, in a sense, is much like the trademark of medieval times, which gave customers assurance that the tradesman's quality would be replicated for the buyer every time.

Why the increased interest in corporate branding? I believe it's because American business has found itself in serious trouble.

1

Corporations spent much of the last decade moving assets around. The result of this turmoil, buried in their consolidated financial reports, is the shocking fact that without acquisitions and mergers many companies would be limping along at zero or even negative growth. The unintended effect of merger mania, buying sprees, and serial restructuring has been to seriously impair if not destroy the identities of many corporations.

Key publics today are asking tough questions of companies that once boasted well-defined, well-promoted reputations. Questions such as, What does your corporation stand for? Who owns it? What do you sell? What is the quality of your products? Why should I buy from you? Are you helping or harming the environment?

Many of the newly reconstituted companies are beginning to recognize the need to rebuild their reputations. Sometimes they need to develop totally new, even global perspectives: that is, points of view that are adapted to and serve different cultures in the marketplace. Above all, they must learn to move quickly and decisively to implement corporate brands if they expect to survive and thrive in the years to come.

Ironically, the single biggest obstacle to realizing effective corporate branding may be the company's chief executive officer. Too often the CEO does not fully believe in the worth of communications because he does not understand that *the value of corporate brand communications is real and can be measured.*

Although we hope this book will be of significant interest and importance to every executive who wants his or her company to grow, it has been written primarily for the CEO. It is the CEO, after all, who has the power to give a corporate branding program direction, focus, impetus and, certainly not least, adequate funding. Moreover, it is the CEO who is the steward of the corporate brand.

Without the CEO's understanding and full support, a corporate branding program has little chance of success. There is a natural tendency for companies to gravitate toward product brand advertising. Somehow, they believe, the corporate personality will be projected through their products. This is a myopic, unfounded view. Companies must balance product and divisional needs with the imperative of the corporate brand; only the CEO has the clout to accomplish this objective.

Succeeding chapters present case studies of a variety of corporations that use corporate branding to their advantage. The studies are based on a great deal of original research, personal and client experiences, and interviews with corporate leaders.

I examine the thinking of CEOs, board members, corporate communicators, marketing executives, and others in management who use corporate branding to create a unified vision for the company and its products. I show how a company can assess the results and value of corporate branding—its measurable impact on a company's stock price, earnings, and sales.

There is a host of other topics I explore which I hope will provoke your own thinking: corporate branding and the roles of the CEO, board of directors, and employees; the corporate will to grow; applying the core brand in global marketing, small businesses, and cause-related marketing; the need for a corporate communications czar in most companies, and putting interactive media in the service of the corporate brand.

My aim is to make you both analytical and passionate about your corporate brand, which is as important a corporate asset as your people.

James R. Gregory
Stamford, Connecticut

CORPORATE BRANDING AND ITS BOTTOM-LINE IMPACT

CHAPTER ONE

WHAT IS CORPORATE BRANDING?

"Life comes before literature, as the material always comes before the work. The hills are full of marble before the world blooms with statues."
—PHILLIPS BROOKS

Flashback: In 1989, Time Inc., the publishing giant, and Warner Communications Inc., the movie and music company, tripped to the altar. Their marriage gave issue to a behemoth company with a capitalization of more than $15 billion and annual revenue exceeding $10 billion. Alas, the nuptials incurred $16 billion in debt.[1]

To mark the union, Steve Ross, chairman and co-CEO of the merged company, hired one of the world's best design firms to create an eye-catching symbol. In fact the logo featured an eye and ear graphic to signify the sensory receptors of Time Warner's media and entertainment businesses.

And what was the new logo's first application? Before any corporate communications of substance were considered, the effusive Ross had the logo cast into limited edition gold cufflinks for select friends. As it turned out, Ross died soon after and his successor replaced the symbol with a plain vanilla wordmark, consigning the flashy ear and eye logo to the cable company.

A BRAND IN SEARCH OF ITSELF

Despite conducting pre-merger studies on how best to integrate the two companies, insiders say Time Warner made no serious provision to assess the latent emotive power and reputation of the new enterprise—what the promise of Time Warner signified to its customers and constituencies.

Riffle through the company's annual reports, and you will find fashionable buzzwords such as *globalization, vertical and horizontal integration,* and the S-word, *synergy,* punctuating an astonishing parade of take-it-to-the bank brands ranging from Bugs Bunny and *People* magazine to HBO and Hootie and the Blowfish. But as a corporation, brand-rich Time Warner has spoken rarely and reactively, as in its recent counterattack against Rupert Murdoch's fulmination over Time Warner's refusal to carry Fox News channel on their cable systems.

Cut to the present: More than half a decade after its merger, Time Warner has not only failed to pay down its debt, it has borrowed heavily to fund more acquisitions, it has never turned a profit, and its stock missed the trajectory of the 1990s bull market. Though its stable of brands remains vigorous, The Brand, the company itself, has not convincingly defined itself—which, I suspect, figures in its performance.

Like many companies, Time Warner is a corporate brand in search of itself.

THE COMPANY'S "LOOK"

All too often, corporate CEOs sanction simplistic approaches to portraying the essence of their companies. There's a mindset that says, "Just change my name, slap a new logo onto the building, announce that 'We Are Born' in a one-time-only, full-page ad in *The Wall Street Journal,* and we're in business. What more do we need to do?"

The norm for many companies about to be born, or born again through structural change, is to fashion a new *corporate identity,* i.e., the company's visual expression—its name, logo, colors, and nomenclature system. Corporate identity is generally concerned with the "look" of a corporation, with affirming an organization's sense of its self through graphic design and the codification of style. It involves fabricating symbols and even a "tradition" for a company, in the way that new regimes in various countries attempt to legitimize their authority.

This can be problematical. The CEO must ask, Does corporate identity truly relate to my company's business plans and our (sometimes shifting) aspirations? Will imposing an artificial sense of belonging on my employees be credible? Can the identity endure beyond the next major acquisition, which may involve a new line of business with different kinds of employees?

THE CORPORATE IMAGE

Since the era of Oil Trusts, management has fretted over its *corporate image,* or how it is perceived by influentials as disparate as institutional investors and politicos within the Beltway. "We've got to change our image," the CEO intones when the company is in trouble. If corporate identity is how a company looks, corporate image is what audiences think they see.

And what they see are multifarious and discrete corporate communications: verbal and nonverbal, directed and undirected, planned and unplanned. The communication could be a magnanimous management gesture. Or: a receptionist's surliness, the smile on a salesperson's face, a confusing customer invoice, a sudden plunge in the stock price, an industrial accident, the success of a product line. These positive and negative experiences coalesce into an overall perception of the company that is quantifiable.

But as many of the inputs to corporate image are often unplanned, image is not specifically market-oriented. Based on the public's net perception of cues that companies intentionally or accidentally communicate, corporate image is inherently a passive experience.

In the words of Abraham Lincoln's admonition ("you can't fool all of the people all the time"), corporate image can't be "changed" for the duration unless the company truly alters its behavior and persuades its publics that it is a "good" actor or, at least, good enough to satisfy the right audiences.

LIBERATING THE CORPORATE BRAND

Corporations are not just pieces of paper filed in a state capital (more often than not, Wilmington, Delaware). Even the law, in certain ways, treats corporations as individuals, and it can be demonstrated that a corporation has values, beliefs, rituals, aspirations, a personality, a reputation—a *brand.* Individuals—whether a person or a company—can, by managing its behavior, shape its reputations. And like a gifted sculptor who can free a muscular torso from a block of marble, an experienced hand can, with the right tools, liberate the corporate essence—your brand—and leverage it into a long-term annuity.

This is what companies really need and want, if they give it serious thought.

What I term *corporate branding* is at once a more inclusive and more focused concept than either corporate identity or corporate image. At its heart is a purposeful, marketing-oriented communications platform across all business units, product and service brands, media and audiences. Its approach is holistic (more than just the sum of the parts), rather than monolithic (rigidly uniform): a carefully considered integrated strategy that sets standards and policies for shaping the corporate brand. And it works.

HARD-NOSED METHODOLOGY

If you think corporate branding sounds like another empathic excursion into the corporate "soul," let me disabuse you. It is hard-nosed in its methodology and hard-edged in its resultant data. Corporate branding systematically elicits inputs from company employees and intimate observers to delineate "who we are" and "what we believe." The information is crafted into essential distinguishing messages (not ad copy) and positionings which can be tested for accuracy and credibility in the marketplace. Reflecting these findings, a comprehensive communications program is designed to impart a specific impression on a target audience. The program can be benchmarked, and measured for financial impact (see Chapter 4).

Corporate branding makes a persuasive statement to a company's customers, its investors, peer companies, the media and, most importantly, its own employees. It provides everyone in the organization with a common goal and works for the cumulative benefit of the corporation by communicating the subtext, "You can believe in our company and in our products."

Increasingly, corporate branding is credited with being a valuable investment in the company's future because it buoys the company's divisions and brands through increased awareness and opportunities for improved cross-selling. Visionary, targeted, controlled, and cost-effective, corporate branding is a dynamic concept: a corporate tool whose time has come.

PROMISES TO KEEP

Observers of corporate branding are in general agreement about how the process works. Writing in *Business Marketing*, Kristin Zhivago makes the salient point that a "brand is not an icon, a slogan, or a mission statement. It is a promise—a promise your company can keep."

"First you find out, using research, what promises your customers want companies like yours to make and keep. Then you figure out what promises you realistically can keep, using the products, processes and people in your company. Then you look at your competition and decide which promise would give you the best competitive advantage.

"This is the promise that you make and keep in every marketing activity, every action, every corporate decision, every customer interaction. You promote it internally and externally.

"The promise drives budgets and stops arguments. If everyone in the company knows what the promise is, and knows that they will be rewarded or punished depending upon their personal commitment to the promise, politics and personal turf issues start to disappear."[2]

THE COMPLETE CORPORATE EXPERIENCE

To express forcefully the essence of the whole corporation, a corporate branding program must influence *all forms* of corporate communications: corporate advertising, brand advertising, media relations, investor relations, customer service, employee communications, and more. Corporate branding *subsumes* corporate identity. It puts the manifestations of identity in service of the brand, including the company's name, symbols and logotype, and nomenclature system. In addition, the corporate brand may be reflected in the company's societal concerns (Patagonia and the environment) or by the style of its architecture and decor (Microsoft and Nike, for example), if these are intended to create a specific impression.

Corporate branding is the complete corporate ethos and experience summed up in the company's reputation and consciously projected to select audiences. By linking the corporate name closely (and showing evidence for the linkage) with such favorable attributes as quality, value, dependability, innovation, community-mindedness, good management, environmental consciousness, and so on, corporate branding builds a special relationship with target audiences. It can change behavior toward the company. With respect to the competition, all other things being equal, corporate branding can be the tie-breaker that motivates people to invest in the corporation, buy its products, recommend it to others, or seek employment there.

In a corporate branding program, the receptionist described earlier would be encouraged to be polite, written corporate communications would be made readable, unusual stock performance would be clearly and promptly explained. Employees would be made aware of the consequences of displaying inappropriate corporate cues, however great or small, and of their cumulative impact on the corporate brand.

What I call corporate branding transcends corporate image and corporate identity. It is a carefully planned, integrated program that shapes desired opinions and prompts positive behavioral responses from targeted audiences—a thoroughly marketing-oriented approach that can contribute to the corporation's marketing success and financial performance.

THE MOST ENDURING BRAND OF ALL?

It can be argued that the concept of corporate branding is not all that novel. Maybe so. There are antecedents in history. Consider the Roman Catholic Church, which knows with certainty what it is about. Goals and a shared system of beliefs, not to mention the vision, are communicated thoroughly throughout its spiritual community. "Amongst the most intricate, complex and ritualized uses of symbolism are those which occur within Christianity," design consultant Wally Olins has observed.[3]

Early on, the Church integrated the cross, perhaps the most powerful of symbols, into the process of worship. It developed rituals, introduced special vestments, and used complex, impressive titles within a carefully ordered naming structure. No organization has better leveraged symbolism, architecture, music, and language to make a continuing impact on its constituency. Its "brand" accommodates growth. Religious orders (the Jesuits, for example) may arise within the "corporate brand," yet everyone remains on message.

A robust, disciplined overarching brand, the Church endures because it periodically updates itself to keep relevant. (To be sure, this exaggerated analogy is meant to instruct, not offend.)

THE EMERGENCE OF CORPORATE BRAND

In recent years the corporate brand has emerged as a major force in advertising and other corporate communications. Product brands remain no less important, but it is becoming increasingly difficult for many consumers to separate corporate and product brands in their minds when making purchase decisions.

As a consequence, we see product brands assuming a secondary role, with growing reliance on the corporate brand to communicate important messages. As customers come to know the corporate persona better than its product brands, it will be imperative to leverage the assets of the corporate brand to the fullest. Some of the most successful companies make great use of their corporate name as part of their overall branding strategy—among them, American Express, Avon, AT&T, IBM, Kodak, General Electric, and CIGNA. Here are précis of how and why two companies enhanced their corporate brands.

FILLING THE BLUE BOX WITH MEANING

CIGNA Corporation is a leading provider of health care, insurance, and financial services. It has 45,000 employees worldwide and assets of about $96 billion. The company was formed in 1982, the result of the merger of Connecticut General and INA. It adopted as its symbol a "blue box" logo, which enclosed the CIGNA acronym, made up of the merged companies' initials. By 1993, the blue box was virtually empty of meaning.

"We were an unknown," says Ed Faruolo, assistant vice president for corporate marketing. "Not to the business audience, but to their employees, the end-users who would select us for medical coverage and other employee benefits. We had an identity problem with our pension business, too . . . . The employer doesn't want their employees coming back and saying, 'Who is this company?'"

Management interviews indicated that CIGNA's image and identity did not reflect company values. A quantitative study of 1,800 consumer and business decision-makers uncovered low to moderate awareness levels. There was also limited understanding of the company's many products: group life, property-casualty insurance, individual life and health insurance, reinsurance products, and investment management. "Regarding image, it was said that although we were solid and stable in a business sense, we were not good in terms of being customer-focused or responsive," Faruolo says.

But therein lay an opportunity: a glass half-full rather than half-empty. "We could build on our strengths as a solid, stable, professional organization, and mold a company that was more responsive, more human, more caring in what we do." The findings led to the development of CIGNA's current symbol, the Tree of Life, and a new identifier, "A Business of Caring," to communicate the company's attributes and evolving philosophy (Exhibit 1–1).

The branding program was promoted vigorously to the public through advertising and to CIGNA's employees via human resource efforts such as employee incentive programs. Concludes Faruolo: "It's helping to change the momentum and customer focus of people throughout the company. It helps shape important attitudes, our own and our customers', and is a very compelling story."

EXHIBIT 1—1A   COMMON THEMES LINK CIGNA ADS FOR THREE BUSINESS LINES

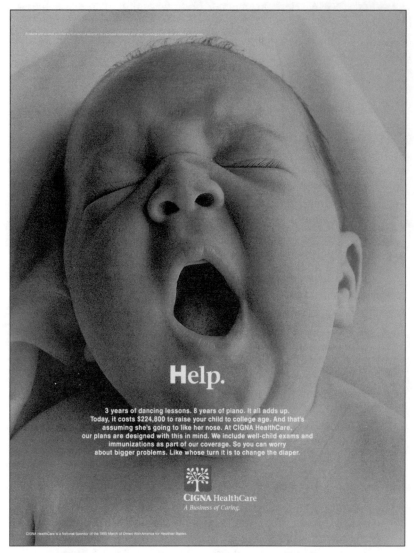

COURTESY OF CIGNA

THE VALUE DECADE

How does a company which operates in more than 100 countries, employs nearly a quarter of a million people and had a market value, at year-end 1995, of $132 billion, largest in the world, initiate an effective corporate branding program? With a lineage dating to

EXHIBIT 1–1B   COMMON THEMES LINK CIGNA ADS FOR THREE BUSINESS LINES

Help.

Fire departments. Ambulances. Rescue squads.
The people who put themselves on the line every day to protect our families and communities. Did you ever stop and wonder who protects them? At CIGNA, we've been insuring heroes for 200 years. Not only helping people in the event of an accident. But always looking for ways to prevent one. After all, we want to sleep nights, too.

CIGNA Property & Casualty
A Business of Caring.

COURTESY OF CIGNA

Thomas A. Edison, General Electric, the only company listed continually on the Dow Jones Industrial Index since its inception in 1896, understands staying power and growth and value.

John F. Welch, chairman and CEO of GE since 1981, offers this advice: "First of all, define your company's vision and its destiny in

EXHIBIT 1—1C   COMMON THEMES LINK CIGNA ADS FOR THREE BUSINESS LINES

COURTESY OF CIGNA

broad but clear terms. Second, maximize your productivity. Finally, be organizationally and culturally flexible enough to meet massive change."[4]

GE communicates its value especially well to the leaders of its twelve major diversified technology, manufacturing and services companies. Management is exhorted to "create a clear, simple, reality-based, customer-focused vision" and to "communicate it straightforwardly to all constituencies."

Specific kinds of behavior are promoted in the organization, including setting aggressive targets and rewarding employee progress; a passion for excellence and disdain for bureaucracy; an openness to "ideas from anywhere"; a sensitivity to diversity and globalism; an invitation to stimulate and accept change. "Possess a mindset that drives quality, cost and speed for a competitive advantage." This is a highly coveted management value.[5]

According to Welch, we are now in what is becoming known as the Value Decade, propelled by a public desire to realize increased value. If you can't sell a top-quality product at the lowest price, you're out of the game.

Fortunately, marketing, still artful but increasingly more empirical, is keeping pace with the needs of the Value Decade. Hunch and hope are giving way to well-honed tools to meet the challenges of today's and tomorrow's marketplace. Undoubtedly, one of the key tools is corporate branding.

Corporate branding campaigns are highly visible and potentially powerful. They concentrate the combined firepower of product brand advertising, corporate advertising, and public and investor relations on delivering a unified company message. If corporate branding is done well, the corporation's prized publics will listen and respond positively. If executed exceedingly well, customers and investors will reward the strong corporate brand. For applied over time, a corporate branding program is a very effective way to increase market share and lift the reputation of the company. And, as we shall see, improved reputation can lead to improved stock performance.

NOTES

1. Connie Bruck, *Master of the Game* (New York: Simon & Schuster, 1994).
2. "Branding? My CEO just doesn't 'Get It,'" Kristin Zhivago, *Business Marketing,* October 1994.
3. Wally Olins, *Corporate Identity* (Thames and Hudson), 1989.
4. "GE's Jack Welch Speaks His Mind," *Point of View,* published by Spencer Stuart Executive Search Consultants, Winter 1993.
5. "Our Management Values," GE, 1996.

CHAPTER TWO

THE CORPORATE BRANDING INDEX: ATTAINING THE "HOLY GRAIL"

"The more complicated the world gets, the more comforting the familiar will seem, and the better it will get for brands."
    — *FORTUNE* MAGAZINE, FEBRUARY 5, 1996

In the hard-nosed business climate of the 1990s, merely asserting the value of corporate branding doesn't win converts among senior management. Touchy-feely concepts and argument couched in language lifted from self-help manuals will not improve corporate self-esteem or pry budget dollars from the CEO to give it a try. Before the CEO springs for a corporate branding program, he will want, and deserves, hard evidence that leveraging a company's brand can truly affect business for the good—and for the long term. What will it cost to manage the corporate brand? What's the return on my investment?, the CEO rightly asks.

Now, for the first time, there are data that link corporate branding with increased sales, increased market share, increased earnings, and increased stock price.

In 1993 Richard Costello of GE and Rupert Smith of GTE, representing the Association of National Advertisers (ANA), asked me to investigate how corporate advertising affects corporate reputation and financial performance. It was THE goal—practically a "Holy Grail"—sought by practitioners of corporate communications for as long as I can remember. Working collaboratively and focusing, initially, on more than half the *Fortune* 100 companies over a seven-year period, we developed a new valuable tool:

> It is called The Corporate Branding Index®, a systematic method of measuring the impact of corporate, brand, and trade advertising on corporate reputation and financial performance over a specific time period.[1]

The Corporate Branding Index reflects the interplay of the level of advertising in support of a corporate brand, knowledgeable assessments of the company's reputation, and the company's actual financial outcomes. While not an indicator of consumer behavior, the Index goes a long way toward providing business executives with answers to the nagging question, "Did my investment in advertising pay off?"

Our specific assignment for ANA was to identify the characteristics of effective corporate and/or brand image advertising and determine how they can be measured. In addition to ANA data, we compiled research from many sources such as *Fortune*, *Business Week*, *The Wall Street Journal*, and Leading National Advertisers, among others. The following summarizes our findings.

THE DRIVERS OF REPUTATION

First we grouped the *Fortune* 100 companies by the degree their reputations changed over the period measured. Then, calculating the ratio of the companies' investment in advertising to company sales, we found that the ratio was highest for companies with the greatest reputation improvement. Companies with the most improved reputations also did the most advertising of the corporate brand. As the advertising-to-sales ratio declined, so too did company reputation. Significantly, the companies with the best reputations experienced the highest earnings growth and best stock performance (Exhibit 2–1).

But looking at company reputation from just one perspective was not enough. We wanted to be able to triangulate the drivers of reputation. We had to discover whether earnings growth was driving reputation or if advertising played the critical role. Which of these was cause, which was effect?

EXHIBIT 2–1   REPUTATION DRIVERS OVER A SEVEN-YEAR PERIOD

Reputation Changes	Ad-to-Sales Ratio	% Earnings Growth	% Stock Growth
Significantly Improved	2.84	272	665
Somewhat Improved	2.68	225	434
Little Changed	1.33	136	345
Somewhat Declined	0.48	67	158
Significantly Declined	0.28	31	131

To find out, we created a "change index," in order to compare companies in different industries. This enabled us to compare a food-processing company to a steel company to an automobile manufacturer, etc. In this way, we could uncover the most successful business practices, irrespective of industry, and identify the drivers of reputation.

In the following discussion, and in the charts from Exhibits 2–2 through 2–7, advertising includes all corporate, brand, and trade advertising in support of the corporate brand, represented by a light gray line. Our measure of reputation, which is based on a proprietary formula using our proprietary data base, is indicated by a dark line. The financial measurement, a black line, reflects revenue, earnings, and stock performance. When these lines are plotted simultaneously over time, various corporate behavioral profiles emerge.

MARKETING-ORIENTED GROWTH COMPANIES

Exhibit 2–2 shows what we call "Marketing-Oriented Growth" companies. Of the *Fortune* 100 companies we studied, about ten percent displayed "Marketing-Oriented Growth" characteristics. The sequential pattern for these companies suggests that stepped-up advertising drives reputation, which in turn helps pull up financial performance. In this formulation, for example, it would have been shortsighted to slash advertising budgets in the first year when financials declined because reputation requires time to repair.

EXHIBIT 2–2   A MARKETING-ORIENTED GROWTH COMPANY

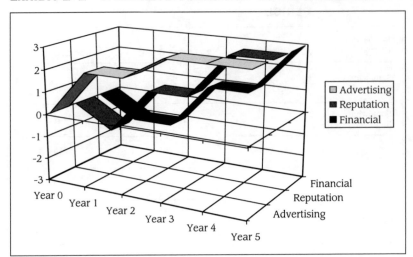

ERRATIC BEHAVIOR

Forty-five percent of the companies we studied—the largest category—displayed "erratic behavior" in terms of their advertising investment (Exhibit 2–3). "Erratics" show no serious commitment to advertising. They will advertise for a year, cut back, advertise again, cut back again, ad infinitum. In the short term, their reputations or financials spike up and down like a diminishing row of ripsaw teeth. But long term, their on-again, off-again advertising leads to a slide in both reputation and financial performance. Erratic Behavior can be a formula for disaster.

THE DEATH SPIRAL

The Death Spiral describes companies that, when suffering financially, cut back their advertising budgets year after year, only to reinforce the financial decline (Exhibit 2–4). They may experience a financial rebound at some point two or three years out, but they don't restore advertising to a level that can make any impact. Once locked into the Death Spiral, it is difficult for a company to recover because the prospect of getting bigger advertising budgets from management is often bleak. Thus it becomes very hard to recoup reputation. To halt the nose-dive, the company's top management invariably is changed.

EXHIBIT 2–3   A COMPANY DISPLAYING ERRATIC BEHAVIOR

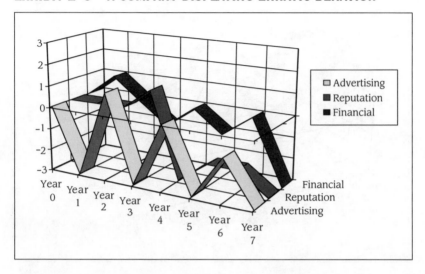

EXHIBIT 2–4   A COMPANY IN THE "DEATH SPIRAL"

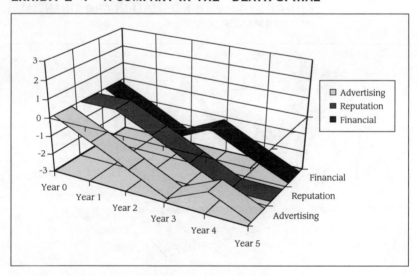

FINANCIALLY DRIVEN COMPANIES

Another category comprises what we call "financially driven" companies—banks, insurance companies, and utilities, for example (Exhibit 2–5). These companies advertise when they've had a good year financially, but tend to cut back in anticipation of unsatisfactory financial results. They are willing to spend on advertising—they

EXHIBIT 2–5   A FINANCIALLY DRIVEN COMPANY

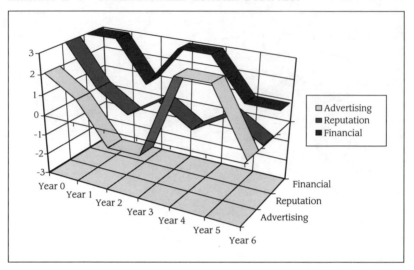

**EXHIBIT 2–6   A FINANCIAL INSTITUTION WITH ADVERTISING
OUT OF SYNC WITH REPUTATION AND FINANCIAL
PERFORMANCE**

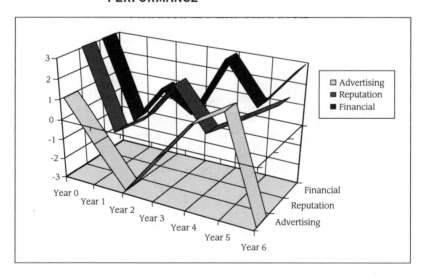

just don't spend it wisely, a pattern evident in many companies. This
kind of advertising behavior does not help drive reputation or financial performance. An extreme example of advertising that is totally
out of sync with both reputation and performance is shown in
Exhibit 2-6, the Corporate Branding Index of a particular financial
institution.

Reputation and Stock Price

Using the Corporate Branding Index model, we have identified a variety of other patterns: companies responding to major crises, companies launching new consumer products, and more. By and large, there is a strong correlation between the level of corporate advertising and reputation. But that's only part of the story.

We have also found that product advertising affects corporate cash flows and stock price in one way; corporate advertising affects corporate familiarity and favorability and the cash flow multiple in another way. Our studies are a work in progress, but we've already learned that the dynamic of corporate branding differs for every major industry:

Depending on the industry, we discovered that reputation accounts for 5 percent, on average, of the stock price. In a game where every advantage must be exploited to stay competitive, leveraging shareholder value 5 percent or so is well worth a company's efforts to enhance their reputation.

What's more, improvements in company reputation can concomitantly boost sales and contribute to employee and customer satisfaction. The volume of internal and external communications generated by most companies represents an untapped resource to shape the corporate brand.

How Corporate Advertising Enhances Shareholder Value

In our work helping companies understand the bottom-line impact of corporate reputation, we use the "linkages" model shown in Exhibit 2–7.

(First, two definitions: Corporate image is comprised of familiarity—how well relevant audiences know your company—and favorability—how well they regard the company in terms of specific qualitative attributes such as its ability to innovate or the quality of its management.)

The linkages model traces two paths between corporate communications and shareholder value. One path—which goes from corporate communications through corporate image and then through business results, i.e., company sales, earnings, and cash flow—receives the lion's share of management attention. After all,

**EXHIBIT 2–7   LINKAGES BETWEEN CORPORATE
COMMUNICATIONS AND STOCK PRICE**

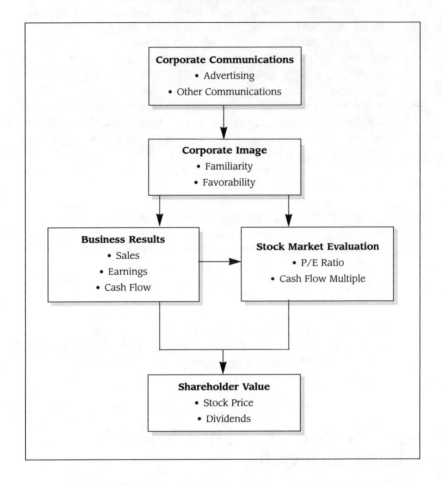

generating revenues, earnings, and cash is crucial to corporate survival and success.

We believe, however, that many companies do not focus sufficiently on the other route—one which flows from corporate communications through corporate image and then to stock market
evaluation, or the P/E ratio and cash flow multiple.

Our findings suggest that corporate image is a potent factor in
the way investors assign a "premium" or "discount" to a company's
stock price via the cash flow multiple. The cash flow multiple is the
stock price divided by cash flow per share of common stock—a construct analogous to the price/earnings ratio. We use cash flow in
addition to earnings because cash flow is more stable, less likely to

be a negative number, and is a better measure of a company's financial health than net income.

In our analysis, we compare a subject company with its competitors and/or similar companies it has selected for benchmarking purposes. In order to quantify the relationships (a) between corporate brand advertising and image, and (b) between image and the cash flow multiple, two sets of numbers are identified: measurements of the company's image, made by people who invest for all companies being compared, and the comparative advertising data for the companies in question.

Using cross-sectional analysis (points in time) and longitudinal analysis (trends over time), we generally find positive linkages in both (a) and (b) above, though the strength of the relationships can vary considerably. And while advertising does exert a positive effect on image, the impact on image tails off as advertising approaches saturation levels.

Relating image to the cash flow multiple requires accounting for important financial and performance factors that influence the cash flow multiple. Analyzing our proprietary data base of hundreds of companies, we are able to attribute as much as 87 percent of the variance in cash flow multiples to such factors as expected cash flow growth, financial strength, level of debt, past price growth, earnings predictability, and price stability. Once these factors were accounted for, we could test whether corporate image has any additional effect on the cash flow multiple.

This was accomplished by comparing the actual cash flow multiple with an "expected value," a figure we developed from a proprietary statistical regression equation that weights financial and performance factors. Across 47 companies, we found a reasonably strong relationship between the actual cash flow multiple (as a percent of expected value) and relative company image. The linkage indicates that image (or an investor's "feelings" and perceptions) is indeed an important factor in how investors value a company through its stock price.

We have developed a computer simulation model to test how alternate levels of corporate brand advertising will likely affect future cash flow multiples and stock prices. Typically, our benefit/cost analyses find a 2:1 to 10:1 benefit from incremental investments in the corporate brand. That is to say, that over a period of five or so years—a reasonable time frame in which to build a company reputation—companies can leverage their total market capitalization by a factor of 2:1 to 10:1, vis-à-vis their total corporate brand investment.

To recap the key findings of The Corporate Branding Index studies:

- There's a strong, positive correlation between corporate reputation and the level of corporate brand advertising.
- Companies that are more aggressive in their corporate brand advertising generally have the highest improvement in their reputation.
- Total corporate advertising, in combination with earnings and stock performance, drives corporate reputation.
- Reputation accounts for perhaps 5 percent of a company's stock price.
- The aggregate value of a company's stock, in relation to the amount invested in its corporate brand communications, can be leveraged from 2:1 to 10:1 in approximately five years.
- Corporate communications is not fully exploited by many companies to build the corporate brand.

NOTE

1. All models used in The Corporate Branding Index are proprietary.

CHAPTER THREE

THE MULTIPLIER EFFECT ON FINANCIAL PERFORMANCE

"We were getting shareholder proposals that were disruptive and creating tension. We want to have love-ins with our shareholders; we don't want to have fights."

—JAMES M. HERRON
SENIOR EXECUTIVE VICE PRESIDENT
RYDER SYSTEMS INC.

Understanding corporate branding, its uses and values in the marketplace, is increasingly necessary for every company, large and small. Corporate branding is the state-of-the-art means of corporate positioning, for now and into the twenty-first century. It is especially worthwhile for a company searching for its identity, struggling to make an impact in the marketplace, finding a need to differentiate itself from competition, undergoing significant changes such as merger, acquisition, divestiture, or spin-off, or has simply lost forward momentum.

Corporate branding is a state of mind; merely thinking and talking about it can help you operate more efficiently by coordinating all your communications, internal as well as external, with a consistent, clear, and purposeful message.

The big question is, How does one determine its real value? Can we be sure that the dollars invested in a corporate brand communications program are having a positive effect on the company's bottom line?

Many executives are skeptical about the bottom-line value of advertising. It is relatively easy for them to measure the success and value to the company of a sales representative, but advertising is less tangible. How do you evaluate its results meaningfully? Executives want hard proof that advertising can be linked causally to increased sales, increased market share, increased profits, or increased stock price.

CORRELATION BETWEEN REPUTATION AND ADVERTISING

Advertising can be measured. First, however, we must understand that in some ways corporations are no different from individuals. Most people strive to manage their reputations so that others will react in a positive manner toward them. Corporations do likewise, knowing that customers and other key audiences often make vital decisions—such as buying, investing, applying for employment, supporting favorable legislation, offering support in proxy fights, and so on—based on corporate reputation.

As already outlined in Chapter 2, studies I conducted for the Association of National Advertisers indicate a strong, positive correlation between corporate reputation and the level of the company's advertising. But how does this affect sales, stock price, and other financial performance?

What, for example, drives the stock price of a company? We know that the main drivers of valuation, and thus stock price, are financial in nature—earnings, cash flow, and so on. But there are other drivers, perhaps difficult to translate into financial terms, but crucial nonetheless. These include management effectiveness, new product development, market position, and, certainly not least, corporate reputation.

What drives reputation? Earnings and stock performance do, of course, but also advertising. When we studied the advertising to sales ratio for Fortune 100 companies (see Chapter 2), we found that total advertising expenditures as a percentage of sales were highest in those corporations with the greatest improvement in reputation. This held true for companies in all three groupings: high, average, and low. The higher the total advertising expenditure, the better the stock performance.

THE QUICKEST PAYBACK

It should come as no surprise that one of the most effective and quickest-payback communications tools used to establish a corporate brand and corporate reputation is advertising. Our corporate branding work for ANA, as well as a variety of studies indicate a strong, positive correlation between corporate reputation—or corporate brand awareness—and the level of advertising. They also show that the earnings growth and stock performance are often higher among companies with the highest advertising budgets as a percentage of sales.

The strategic framework of investor relations should maintain a special place for advertising, not merely for reaching individuals but also for building an awareness and image among institutions, stock brokers, and sell-side analysts. A number of studies show that advertising influences these audiences to become more aware of a company, take a look at its stock, and learn about the significant changes that can lead to an investment decision. In fact, portfolio managers often purchase a stock after initially becoming familiar with the company through its advertising.

From *Update:* "Hanson Industries, the eighth largest company in terms of marketing cap on the London exchange, is using corporate advertising aggressively in creating higher levels of awareness and knowledge of the company as part of a strategy to increase substantially the number of shares held by U.S. investors, both individual and institutional. To date, more than 29,000 requests for annual reports have resulted from the ongoing campaign."[1]

THE RELATIONSHIP BETWEEN ADVERTISING AND GROWTH

A three-year study conducted by the International Data Group (IDG) has found that there is indeed a link between advertising and brand awareness, market share, profitability, and other critical measures. Commissioned to assess advertising's effects in the computer industry, the IDG research showed that the companies that sustain higher relative levels of advertising produce higher growth in both revenue and profits.

Revenue growth of high-volume print advertisers, even after correction for inflation, was more than double that of low-volume advertisers. Findings on earnings were even more dramatic. High-volume advertisers' profit margins grew at more than four times the rate of low-volume advertisers. Overall, the low-volume advertisers were estimated to allocate less than 1 percent of their total sales to all advertising, while the high-volume advertisers invested about 4.5 percent.

BUILDING BRAND AWARENESS AND APPROVAL

The first job of corporate advertising must be to build corporate brand awareness and, equally important, corporate brand approval, even preference. Thirty years of American Business Press (ABP) case histories and research studies support this concept and show that advertising can make both consumer and business-to-business marketing more profitable.

For many advertisers, generating strong brand approval and preference is more critical than generating leads. This is particularly so for advertisers who have little or no control over the sales follow-up process. They may sell through manufacturers' reps, distributors, or other sales organizations. This doesn't mean, of course, that you can't generate leads with corporate advertising. You can, and should! Asks *The Financial Times:*

> *What makes a company buy a computer system from a particular manufacturer when a dozen others produce systems at competitive price and similar specification? How do you differentiate yourself?*
>
> *Your company frequently is the brand, and your customers' views about the company will often determine whether they place an order with you or with one of your competitors. In this situation, perhaps the most important awareness to be cultivated is your public reputation as a company, not just as a provider of individual products.*
>
> *Why would you buy from (one particular) computer company? Is it not because you have gradually become aware that behind their products lies a large, credible organization offering support, service, and commitment to research and development?*[2]

IMPROVING FINANCIAL PERFORMANCE

As our ANA Corporate Branding Study indicates, corporate brand advertising can help improve financial performance. Stock performance, for example, was highest among companies with the highest advertising budgets as a percentage of sales. Earnings growth

Five Ways to Assess Brand Value

In his book, *Managing Brand Equity,* David A. Aaker, professor of marketing strategy at the University of California at Berkeley, discusses the need for determining the value of a brand, along with five ways to do it:

"Placing a value on a brand is important for several reasons. . . . Since brands are bought and sold, a value must be assessed by both buyers and sellers. Investments in brands in order to enhance brand equity need to be justified, as there are always competing uses of funds. A bottom line justification is that the investment will enhance the value of the brand. . . .

"At least five general approaches to assessing the value of brand equity have been proposed. One is based on the price premium the name can support. The second on the impact of the name on customer preference. The third looks at the replacement value of the brand. The fourth is based on stock price. The fifth focuses on the earning power of a brand."[3]

In every case, the use of corporate advertising and other corporate communications can exert a positive influence on the value being measured.

---

generally followed the same trend. Revenue growth also followed but not as consistently.

The same trends held true when we examined individual companies within the grouped categories. The higher the advertising to sales ratio, the greater the stock and earnings performance. Revenue followed suit, but to a lesser degree.

When focusing on individual companies, we discovered some interesting anomalies. Some companies seem to spend enough to merit a higher reputation category of performance but don't make it, while others spend less than would seem necessary and still reach a higher level of performance.

The primary difference between these companies is that those which devote a significant part of their total budgets to corporate advertising tend to reach higher performance levels. While the data base here is small and therefore highly speculative, it appeared that the higher the level of investment in corporate advertising, the higher the level of corporate brand awareness achieved and the better the financial performance.

"LIKE GROWING ASPARAGUS"

Cultivating corporate reputations requires patience, but it's worth the effort. Comments Jim Foster, chairman and CEO of Brouillard Communications:

> We often can tell, for instance, whether we have doubled the number of analysts following a company's stock or enhanced acceptance of a product line outside a company's established area of perceived competence.
>
> Forty-five major companies, in nine industries, were examined in terms of their reputations. If their scores were a five or six on a six-point scale, they were classified as winners. We then asked: Suppose you are investing $75,000 . . . how much would you invest in [each company in turn]? The average for companies they rated as winners was twice what they would invest in non-winners.
>
> On October 19,1987, `Black Monday', winners dropped 18 percent on average; non-winners fell 23 percent on average—the same as Dow and S&P. On the following day, winners rebounded 5 percent, while non-winners rose only 2 percent on average. What should be obvious is that a good reputation significantly impacts the bottom line.
>
> You never know when you're going to need a good reputation to fall back on; so corporate advertising is a lot like growing asparagus. When you need it, you find you should have started years earlier.[4]

FORM AND SUBSTANCE

My "Survey of Financial Analysts' Attitudes toward Corporate Image and Communications" shows that clear and timely corporate communications play a very important role for 80 percent of the financial analysts questioned. Yet, according to their answers, only 25 percent of the companies they follow offer those clear and timely corporate communications. Moveover, only 30 percent of the senior managements surveyed were rated as consistently doing a good job of articulating the vision of their corporations. Obviously, there is room for improvement in the area of investor relations.

Form and substance are basic to investor relations. If form is the media selected—annual reports, direct mail, sophisticated presentations, and the like—then substance is the realization that enormous leverage can be obtained by articulating a clear, concise and consistent message to all key audiences.

Valuation is now taking center stage in corporate strategic thinking and the investor relations process. Quoting the National Investor Relations Institute's *Update:*

> *Companies are being encouraged to study the evidence on how stock prices and investors behave, applying the knowledge in programs geared to raise share price and thus maximize shareholder value.*
>
> *In so doing, there are two major roles for investor relations people: using their relationships with institutions and understanding of how the securities markets operate to advise management on share price enhancement programs; and communicating the programs to favorably disposed investor segments.*
>
> *The notion of carving corporate strategies for the primary purpose of influencing stock price can be called the new school of investor relations, honed mainly over the last decade.[5]*

How far should companies go in deliberately developing strategies with higher shareholder value as the main objective? Certainly as far as the creation of a corporate branding program. Although not the only means a company may use to influence share price, corporate branding can be one of the most cost effective. By enhancing corporate reputation, corporate branding can build a special relationship with analysts and investors, as well as with other target audiences. It can motivate them to positive action, often leading to an improved stock performance.

FOCUSED ON THE FUTURE

The corporate themes and messages "most attractive in evaluating companies," according to our Financial Analysts Attitudes Survey, are what we call corporate branding messages. These messages are not based on financial performance alone. They are visionary and marketing oriented—focused on future sales and earnings, company standing versus competition, meeting customer needs, and commitment to quality. At the bottom of the scale are corporate history (a favorite of many CEOs), environmental policies, and advocacy messages although each of the latter two can be extremely effective with the right audience. (See Chapter 11.)

The most important roles of corporate advertising noted by the survey respondents were to increase awareness and to create a positive selling attitude—both products of corporate branding. When asked if advertising or media has ever influenced analysts to research a company in depth, an astounding 50 percent said yes.

An increasing number of companies are more aggressive now in describing the key factors that determine their stock variation. Their corporate branding messages are beginning to have more direct influence in the market's pricing of their shares, motivating both analysts and investors positively.

MANAGE EXPECTATIONS WISELY

"In helping shape valuation, it is important to manage expectations accurately," says Peter Crawford, Bell Atlantic executive director of investor relations. In so doing, Bell Atlantic seeks to match closely its internal business plan with external expectations, and for good reason. "The market doesn't like businesses that fall short of expectations on a continuing basis," he says.

As part of the valuation formula, Crawford seeks constant feedback from the investment community through surveys that include focus group sessions. "Getting feedback on a continuing basis is the single most important factor in putting together the right messages and making the right moves," he says.[6]

Crawford also studies the qualitative factors driving valuation, adding that management is highly interested in knowing them. He estimates that he probably spends 40 percent of his time interpreting issues and market concerns for his management. It's time well spent, he believes.

BRAND BUILDING PAYS OFF FOR STOCKHOLDERS

Investors pay serious attention to corporate branding messages. David A. Aaker and Robert Jacobson write:

> *Our research shows that brand building for 34 major U.S. corporations did pay off where it really counts in our system—for the shareholder.*

Managers are under pressure to deliver results enhancing current-term financial measures. This pressure is largely driven by the need to meet shareholders' objectives and the realization that current-term financials affect stock price.

Will creating and maintaining a strong brand identity pay off? Will investors appreciate strategies designed to enhance brand equity? Our research now makes clear that changes in brand equity do affect stock return. We examined the extent to which brand equity provides information about firm performance that influences stock prices above and beyond that contained in current-term return on investment (ROI).

We found, as widely acknowledged, that stock return is positively related to changes in ROI. But, remarkably, we also found that changes in brand equity matter, too. While not quite as large as responses to ROI, our results depict a strong positive association between brand equity and stock return. Firms experiencing the largest gains in brand equity saw their stock return average 30 percent. Conversely, those firms with the largest losses in brand equity saw stock return average a negative 10 percent.[7]

The linkage between stock return and brand equity should encourage those managers attempting to justify their investments in brand equity. This is especially so when they have to face tough questions about their contribution to the bottom line. American business must do more to communicate such strategies in a way the shareholders can understand and appreciate.

Yankelovich Partners, as well, comes up with similar findings. In conducting a pilot investigation for *Fortune* on "Leveraging Corporate Equity," they determined that one key aspect of behavioral support was that "analysis of the actual stock market price/earnings values of high-, moderate-, and low-equity companies [indicates] a relationship between corporate equity scores in this study and actual P/E ratio. In keeping with claimed likelihood of purchasing a company's stock, higher equity companies actually have substantially higher P/E ratios than moderate or lower equity corporations."

THE ROLE OF PERCEPTIONS

Investor perceptions can be important to a company's stock value. Robert Amen, president of Robert Amen & Associates, points out that "It is important to understand valuation and P/E ratios, but investor relations people have to remember that perceptions are also crucial."[8]

Amen says his firm conducts about 900 interviews with institutional investors on behalf of clients in an average year, and his sense is that while 40 percent of the value of a company may be based on tangible factors such as cash flow and earnings momentum, 20 percent is based on management quality and another 40 percent is based on "perceptions of the future prospects of the industry and the particular company." The implications for corporate branding are clear.

MARKETING TECHNIQUES: THE OPERATIVE CHOICE

Study after study shows that marketing is a key factor in stock price improvement. Companies should approach the task in the same way they market their products. The process of improving stock price involves the development of investor awareness, the establishment of a good image, and getting investors favorably disposed toward the company.

"Those who follow companies today are interested in a far broader range of issues," offers Rob Swadosh, executive vice president and head of investor relations at Golin/Harris.

> They are interested in the objectives behind what a company is doing and in the strategies it hopes to use to accomplish those objectives, but they are also increasingly interested in environmental awareness and whether a company is socially responsible, because those things have implications for the bottom line.
>
> Investor relations has evolved into a marketing discipline rather than a purely financial one. It has to function as a component in the broader discipline of corporate communications. It must work hand-in-hand with public relations on all issues pertaining to the corporate reputation.

It is apparent that more and more investor relations people now recognize the role of market intelligence as a basic tool for conducting IR programs. Information is growing more sophisticated all the time, and companies are getting better at using marketing techniques to identify targets for their securities and determining the information that is crucial for expanding investment interest. Marketing is thus seen as the operative choice in framing and executing investor relations programs.

The company seeking to influence potential investors, says Robert Amen, "needs to develop a unique message. The job of investor relations is increasingly a marketing and communications function, in which the company must separate itself from other corporations and from other investment choices. The executive has to use every available tool—from market research to direct mail, from media relations to effective presentation techniques."[9]

Whatever communications techniques best suit your company's needs, the important point is to establish and promote your own particular corporate brand, thoughtfully and creatively. Its power and efficiency can go a long way toward influencing stock price, thereby convincing the financial analyst and winning the investor.

MOVING THE NEEDLE ON SALES

Impact on stock price is just one advantage of corporate branding, of course. MCI uses it to improve their market share, and they monitor their success with ongoing research.

When the Business Services Division of MCI was formed in August 1992, the unit needed to inform businesses that MCI was at parity with AT&T in terms of service and reliability. According to William Pate, Senior Manager for Advertising for MCI Business Services, "businesses that come to us are always going to be able to save money over AT&T.

"These are the kinds of messages we must be sure businesses know about. We need to correct certain perceptions. One of AT&T's strategies has been to try to confuse the marketplace and hope that people just get apathetic enough not to switch. We needed a campaign that would really break through . . . a campaign that positioned us in such a way that when our reps went to sell, they found open doors. We have been successful in doing that."

MCI did baseline research prior to launching their campaign, and they continue with a program of monthly research—measuring the marketplace, measuring their position, measuring their competitors' positions.

Equally useful is the playback from their field reps. They know how many and which doors are open to them. They can sense the reactions of their prospective customers to MCI's corporate brand program. And they know who is buying.

Continues Pate: "Clearly we are moving the needle on sales and we know that advertising is contributing to that. Continuity is very important. It adds value to the advertising because we gain from the repetitiveness of the message. The very fact that you're out there and advertising every day positions you as a leader.

"We continue to hammer home the message to businesses that it is a two-horse race. As long as they understand that service- and reliability-wise we're at parity with AT&T, it comes down to [which offers] the better price break. And that's how we take share away from AT&T."

REDEFINING THE BRAND IMAGE

What happens when a company's corporate brand no longer seems appropriate to its current marketing situation? Even companies with supposedly solid reputations and strong financials may find it necessary at times to review and recast a corporate brand. Sears did with remarkable success.

"For most of this century," says *The Real World Strategist,* "Sears, Roebuck and Co. was the dominant retailer in America and the nation's most trusted economic institution. Nothing did more to raise living standards than the ubiquitous Sears catalog, the beloved 'wish book'.

"But by the mid-1970s, Sears had turned into a disaster. Retailing revenues declined. Share prices collapsed, from $61 in 1972 to $24 in 1977. By 1991, upstart discounters Wal-Mart and K mart had both passed Sears in sales volume."

This was a problem of an outmoded business definition. Sears needed to redefine its business away from "all things for all people" and focus on those areas where it could offer superior value.[10]

Sears, however, wouldn't sacrifice a single consumer or product segment. Nor would it move from house brands to outside suppliers, thus giving up the manufacturer's markup. It simply did not want to change a corporate branding message that had been successful for the better part of a century.

THE PAIN OF NOT CHANGING

However, when Sears did take action in 1977, it made a major blunder by adopting a business definition that didn't really define a specific corporate position. Ignoring the basic flaw of conglomeration—that there are no real synergies among business units—

Sears decided to become a financial services Goliath and bought stock brokerage Dean Witter Reynolds and real estate brokerage Coldwell Banker, and launched the Discover credit card.

Half-hearted attempts to turn around the stores ended in failure. The dollar investments and the "short-term pain" required to give consumers greater value were more than Sears wished to incur. Its stores declined. Shareholder value was misused and wasted for 20 years—until the pain of not changing was greater than the pain of changing.

Just what brought about Sears' dramatic turnaround? "It took an outsider," comments *The Real World Strategist*, "former Saks Fifth Avenue executive Arthur Martinez, to take control of the situation and start turning it around." Mr. Martinez became head of Sears retail operations in 1992 and began spending $4 billion to remodel out-of-date stores. He also upgraded the merchandise, adding private brand apparel and cosmetics. In effect, he revamped marketing.

Comments *The Real World Strategist:* "Most notably, he axed the sacrosanct but money-losing catalog. He also closed unprofitable stores, mostly smaller, stand-alone stores in small towns and inner cities.

"Martinez understood that a turnaround required focusing like a laser on business definition. Consequently, Sears spun off Coldwell Banker, Dean Witter, the Discover Card, and even 20 percent of venerable Allstate Insurance, and focused on the core merchandising business.

"Since the new definition and strategy were put in place, Sears has led the retail industry in sales gains. During the crucial December 1993 holiday season, 'same store sales' for all major chains were up by 4.3 percent on the Solomon Brothers index. Sears led the pack with a 13.2 gain. At the end of January 1994, Sears stock sold at $55, up 54 percent over its 52-week low."

In 1995, Martinez succeeded the retiring Edward Brennan as CEO. Writes Judith H. Dobrzynski in *The New York Times*, "When retailers released their holiday sales figures, Sears was no longer a laggard. It was the star. In the worst season since the 1990 recession, other big stores posted minimal gains or losses, but Sears registered a 9.2 percent sales increase. Sears, again just a retailer, was back.

"Revenue climbed 5.9 percent to about $35 billion, while net profit probably grew to $995 million, according to a conservative estimate. The company's stock price jumped nearly 71 percent—a gain second only to Merck among the 30 blue-chip stocks in the Dow Jones industrial average."[11]

**EXHIBIT 3–1
ADVERTISEMENT
PROMOTING SEARS'
SPONSORSHIP OF
RINGLING BROS.
BARNUM & BAILEY
CIRCUS**

MEASURING SEARS AS A "GOOD PLACE"

CEO Martinez has made Sears a winner on Wall Street. Now he's out to win back the loyalty of customers. "What he is trying to do," says Dobrzynski, "is foment a cultural revolution, a re-education effort that would make Mao proud. He [wants] to create common ground, to make sure people understand what he's doing.

"'What was good enough to get us where we are is not good enough to get us going forward," Martinez said recently. If employees can be convinced that change is a must, they may alter their behavior willingly and accept Martinez's attempts to decentralize and restructure Sears for growth.

"The effort goes far beyond pep rallies and the company's 'Pure Selling Environment Circuses'—which tie in with Sears' corporate sponsorship of the Ringling Brothers Barnum & Bailey Circus's national tour. It includes discussion groups, training sessions, new job descriptions, new operating structures and a new pay system— all intended to place decision making closer to the customer and make it customer friendly.

"Today's consumers are time-strapped shoppers who have many stores to choose among for whatever they buy. To compete, Sears [has] to provide more service, convenience, and value.

"Sometime in 1994, Sears had gained enough sales momentum for Martinez to focus on corporate culture. 'Sears' fundamental problem was arrogance from past success,' he said. 'That blinded it to what was going on in the competitive arena and with customers.'

"His prescription: 'We have to change how we think about ourselves and what we want to be known for. That's how we came to the three C's.' The three C's is internal shorthand for the overarching theme at Sears. The actual slogan, introduced in 1994, is: 'A compelling place to shop/work/invest.'"[12]

There is a powerful corporate branding message reflected in "The Softer Side of Sears" advertising campaign. It positions Sears as a good place for shoppers and also for workers and investors. It's a message to employees to produce, hit performance targets, and take part in the corporate transformation process. It's also an important step to achieving the financial results that can put Sears among the nation's top performers in the stock market. Finally, it guides Sears well along the road to providing more value to customers, thus attracting more shoppers and getting more of the money they spend.

EXHIBIT 3–2 GTE CORPORATE ADVERTISEMENT

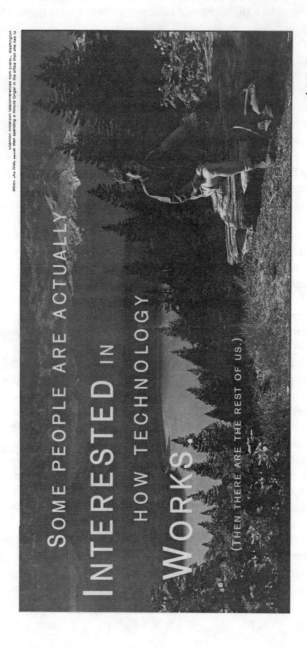

EXHIBIT 3–3 GTE CORPORATE ADVERTISEMENT

DOES CORPORATE BRANDING WORK?

Does corporate branding really work? Can it impact stock price, earnings, revenues, sales, and so on, significantly? We know it can and does. Is it possible to measure that impact honestly and accurately? Our own research, as well as that of others, says that it certainly is possible, and should be done on a continuous basis.

In a recent interview, Ed MacEwen, GTE's Vice President for Corporate Communications, commented:

> *We have done corporate advertising since the early 1970s. As a consequence, we have accumulated years of tracking studies. We run them twice a year on corporate reputation and recognition, particularly measuring corporate attributes like loyalty, value, and so forth.*
>
> *It's very persuasive when you can show major growth in recognition and value. There is always a need for what I would call a door opener. We try to find real life examples of where recognition of GTE has been a specific plus for our sales people where they can get in to see somebody because they were from GTE, even though our salesman might not have been known or the product understood.*
>
> *We have examples like that, and we use them in our budget presentations. Fortunately, we have some people pretty high up in the company's operation who have experienced just that. This is the kind of information—proof of success, if you will—that helps persuade senior management that our brand image advertising and tracking studies are vital, and should be continuous and funded well.*

What works for GTE can work for just about any other company. The need for measurement never really stops. The churn in the marketplace, with new participants always entering, and the change in target audiences as a company's emphasis alters course demand up-to-date research figures. Ongoing, continuous measurement is necessary if corporate management is to control the corporate image.

NOTES

1. National Investor Relations Institute, "Advertising's Role in Investor Relations Strategy," *Update,* April 1995.
2. "Corporate Advertising—Wouldn't You Like to Be Known and Understood?" *Financial Times.*

3. David A. Aaker, *Managing Brand Equity* (The Free Press, Division of MacMillan, Inc., 1991).
4. "Update: Jim Foster at August Meeting," *B/PAA News,* September 1992.
5. National Investor Relations Institute, "New School of Investor Relations: Focusing Strategies on Stock Price," *Update,* April 1990.
6. National Investor Relations Institute, "Valuation Offers Major Opportunity for IR to Add Value to Company," *Update,* October 1994.
7. David A. Aaker and Robert Jacobson, "Study Shows Brand-Building Pays Off for Stockholders," *Advertising Age,* July 18, 1994.
8. Robert A. Amen, "Investor Relationships as Issues Management," *Inside PR,* October 1992.
9. Robert A. Amen, "U.S. Investor Relations Adjusts to Volatile Capital Markets," address to The French Investor Relations Society, May 25,1988, Paris, France.
10. James W. Fullinwider, "Redefined, Sears Makes Comeback," *The Real World Strategist,* 1, No. 1.
11. Judith H. Dobrzynski, "Yes, He's Revived Sears, But Can He Reinvent It?" *The New York Times,* January 7, 1996.
12. Ibid.

How Corporate Branding Is Achieved

CHAPTER FOUR

Crafting the Brand

"What's the reason to trust a company in a new country or in a business it knows nothing about? My God, it's the brand."

—Laurel Cutler, Executive Vice President, Foote Cone & Belding

The scope of corporate branding comprises everything a company says and does. It is an amalgam of corporate utterances, corporate action, and the multitude of corporate cues (unintended body English) described earlier. Most companies possess the working parts of an efficient communications engine—including corporate communications, investor relations, public relations, brand advertising, sales and distribution communications, employee communications, corporate identity, and corporate advertising (Exhibit 4–1). The challenge is to orchestrate these rich disciplines and compartmentalized functions into a purring, powerful engine that can shape the corporate brand.

One Step at a Time

Building the corporate brand is a step-by-step process (Exhibit 4–2). First, you review your company's trove of marketing research data. Sizable companies conduct research, but many don't appreciate the value of the information they have in their data bases. Review your data carefully in order to establish benchmarks to measure progress (or lack of it) in the branding process.

EXHIBIT 4–1   THE SCOPE OF CORPORATE BRANDING

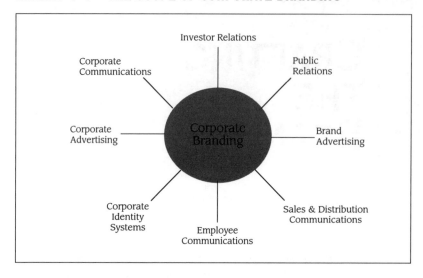

EXHIBIT 4–2   BUILDING YOUR CORPORATE BRAND

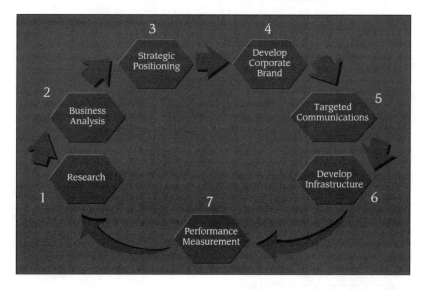

Research all the various constituencies that are important to your company. If you don't set benchmarks for your primary audiences, it will be difficult to prove that their opinion of your company has improved over time. Typical benchmark audiences may include customers, prospects, vendors, employees, investors, financial analysts, the media, opinion-shapers, and government regulators. Additional original research may be required.

Doing the business analysis is the second step. In essence this means setting goals for your communications programs that are based on a thorough understanding of your business objectives. The approach is analytical and verifiable. Various tools can aid you in defining the goals and measuring the brand. We believe that one of the most useful is The Corporate Branding Index, described in Chapter 2. In addition we have developed other measures and analytical approaches that are proving successful, such as the Corporate Brand Advertising Return on Investment Analysis, the Stock TimeLine Index, and Competitive Business Benchmark Analysis.

The third step is to create the strategic positioning document, which distills the central purpose of a company. A single-minded proposition supported by facts, the positioning differentiates you from the competition. It should spring from your corporate strategy, reflect your financial and performance goals, and build on your competitive strengths. Above all, the positioning should be infused by the company's vision. Much depends on this document, for it is the seed crystal for the growth of the corporate brand.

With the branding groundwork laid, you then create a communications platform targeted to key audiences through all the channels the company commands. The platform defines the corporate brand, declaring who you are, what makes your company unique, and what your brand promises. Advertising and public relations professionals, human resources specialists, and others are brought in to create the branding communications, working off the carefully thought-out platform. The next step is to execute the corporate branding program.

A FULLY INTEGRATED PROGRAM

A prerequisite to an effective corporate branding program is ensuring that a communications infrastructure is in place throughout the company's departments and business units. The infrastructure must be able to communicate the corporate brand in a coherent, integrated way. The more decentralized a company is, the more organized its communications must become (Exhibit 4–3).

Discordant, contradictory messages confuse and alienate audiences. Summarily requiring all parts of the company to "increase the signal" of a particular message is counterproductive, too. In

EXHIBIT 4–3   INTEGRATED CORPORATE BRANDING INFRASTRUCTURE

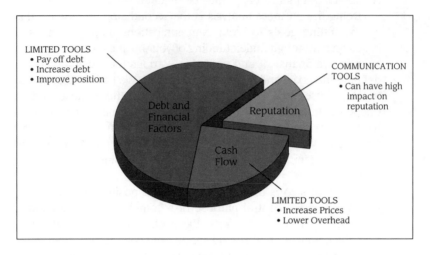

contrast to turning up the volume on one repeatedly struck chord (the corporate message as mantra), the inherent holistic nature of corporate branding calls for harmonious communications. It's about playing variations on a central theme which all the players truly appreciate. Repetitive messages bore; messages working together resonate in a way that is more powerful, more dimensional, more memorable to the audience.

It is therefore important to harness the energy and meld the skills of the company's communications apparatus, from the building custodian to the corporate brand custodian (the CEO). Everyone in the company should be able to tell you in a couple of sentences what the company does, where it's going, what its vision is.

Communications—and communicators—must be viewed in the widest context. For example, sales communications should include direct sales, telemarketing, down-stream sales, and so on. Marketing communications should take into account advertising, media buying, collateral materials, trade shows, and product marketing. Responsibilities must be assigned accordingly so that all the elements of the communications infrastructure work together.

A prime reason for Erratic Behavior in advertising is that communications budgets are fractionalized and not used cohesively throughout the company. If limited by an underpowered budget, corporate advertising will barely make an impression on its intended audiences. And because management doesn't see immediate tangible results, the advertising budget, usually the company's heftiest communications investment, may be reduced or even eliminated. Developing a communications infrastructure not only reinforces essential messages, but modulates management's hierarchical view of communications by locating advertising in a larger communications context.

Performance measurement, the final step in the process, involves additional analytical and market research that compares results with benchmarks and provides management with evidence that goals have been achieved. Successful corporate branding programs have a beginning, but never end. The entire brand-building process should be continuous, like a process control system in a chemical plant.

GETTING EMPLOYEES ON BOARD

As important as advertising and public relations are to a successful corporate branding program, they are not the only powerful communications tools a company has at its disposal. Unique among all elements of corporate branding is the employee force. Employees are a target audience, a channel of communications, and part of the company message itself. Employees can make or break the corporate brand (see "Seeking the 'Branded' Employee," Chapter 7).

Your employees must understand the branding program, must appreciate its importance to the company's (and their own) success, and be fully committed to it. Despite the volume of internal communications available in companies today—so-called top-down communications, bottom-up messages, peer-to-peer communications—as well as new communication technology such as intranets, employees are not a "captive" audience. They have to be convinced through solid reasoning, training, and incentives that the real payoff of corporate branding will be reflected ultimately in their paychecks.

Corporate branding is designed to change attitudes and behavior, the employee's no less than the customer's. At a time when perpetual restructuring is eroding employee loyalty and breeding cynicism, the strong corporate brand bids fair to become a beacon of hope for employees for years to come.

REPUTATION IS THE BRAND

In the end, the brand is the reputation, and the reputation is the brand. An aggressive corporate branding program pervades all the ways a corporation interacts with its constituencies. Its measure of effectiveness is in the company's reputation, stock performance, revenue, and earnings.

Corporate branding helps improve perceptions—and correct misperceptions—of your service, product quality, value, dependability, and innovation. Each time your company, management, products, or employees come in contact with the public represents an opportunity to enhance your reputation. That is why all of the corporation's communications are integral to its marketing success and financial performance.

Speaking to corporate communicators about the corporate brand, Charles Brymer, CEO of Interbrand Schecter, said this:

> We define a brand as a trademark, which to consumers represents a particular and appealing set of values and attributes. It's much more than a product. Products are made in a factory. A product becomes a brand only when it stands for a host of tangible, intangible and psychological factors. A key point to remember is that brands are not created by the manufacturer. They exist only in the eye of the beholder, the customer.[1]

ESTABLISHING A BOND WITH THE CUSTOMER

The customer's eye is suffering from surfeit of commercial messages. Three years ago, Media Dynamics estimated the average adult in the U.S. is bombarded by as many as 247 television ads a day—not to mention the countless signs and billboards selling products and services across the avenues and malls of America.[2]

"The marketplace will continue to become more and more competitive in the future, with a steady escalation in options for consumers," noted Richard Garvey, vice president for marketing at LEGO Systems Inc. LEGO believes its customers, largely parents, "want more than merely to buy a product from a company. They want to understand what that company stands for."

Says Garvey: "We want to create an image for the LEGO brand that will cut through the clutter of competitive offerings and establish a meaningful emotional bond with our consumers. Simply put, we want our customers to buy from us instead of from our competitors."[3]

First created in the little town of Billund, Denmark, LEGO bricks have now spread all over the world. Millions of children, from the United States to Australia and from South Africa to Finland, spend billions of hours a year building an astonishing variety of toys and structures (Exhibit 4–4).

Teachers cleverly employ LEGO toys as instructional aids in the classroom. Therapists working with learning disabled children use LEGO play as a form of nonverbal conceptualizing. Architects and city planners realize their designs in three-dimensional models built out of LEGO bricks. Near Billund, LEGOLAND Park, a 30-acre fantasy land of miniature buildings constructed almost entirely of LEGO bricks, attracts more than one million visitors a year (Exhibit 4–5).

At its U.S. headquarters in Enfield, Connecticut, the LEGO company maintains a child care center (Exhibit 4–6).Open to the public as well as to LEGO employee children, the center resembles a pile of colorful LEGO blocks. Aside from the promotional value of its distinctive appearance, the center offers employees a greater stake in the company by letting them take an active role, on the job, in their children's lives. Involved parents can help plan a curriculum that includes homework assistance and playtime on computers.

By seeking the genuine engagement of their employees in the LEGO brand, the company satisfies a major concern of working parents, distinguishes itself from the competition, and extends the brand in a unique way.

NOTES

1. "The Corporate Brand and the Bottom Line," Charles Brymer, delivered to Corporate Communications Conference, sponsored by the Association of National Advertisers Inc., September 12–14, 1993.
2. "The Brand's the Thing," *Fortune*, February 5, 1996.
3. "Standing Out in a Crowded Field," *The New York Times*, January 17, 1993.

EXHIBIT 4–4   COVER AND SPREAD FROM *THE WORLD OF LEGO TOYS*

Overleaf: The enormous model of the U.S. Capitol draws the biggest crowds and the loudest gasps of surprise. A triumph of craftsmanship in LEGO bricks, the replica was created by Dagny Holm, one of the chief designers in Denmark. It is so large that it must be shipped in sections and assembled at the display site.

LEGO® WORLD SHOW

Models of famous buildings, landmarks, spaceships, and inventions travel around the world to demonstrate that there is no limit to what can be built with LEGO bricks. The models in the LEGO World Shows are painstakingly crafted in shops at Billund, Denmark, and Enfield, Connecticut. The Statue of Liberty is a perennial crowd-pleaser, and viewers are always surprised at the architectural accuracy of such models as Independence Hall.

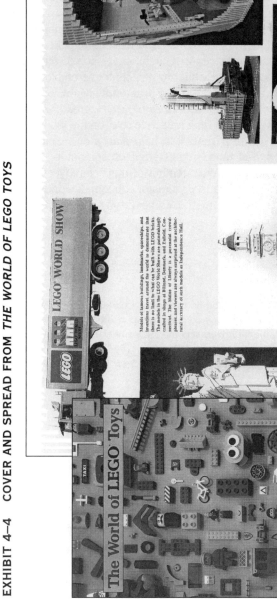

EXHIBIT 4–5   PRESS KIT COVER FOR LEGO'S "INVENTION ADVENTURE"

COURTESY OF LEGO

EXHIBIT 4–6   PAMPHLET ADVERTISING LEGO'S CREATIVE CHILDCARE CENTER

COURTESY OF LEGO

CHAPTER FIVE

ESTABLISHING THE KEY MESSAGE

"The proper goal is to achieve superior quality in areas that matter to the customer. Perdue's secret [of success] is its innovative understanding of the concept of quality. Frank Perdue listened to how the customer defined quality. Then he provided what the customer wanted, and made sure the customer had a chance to learn about—and remember—his quality improvements."

　　—BRADLEY T. GALE
　　FOUNDER
　　CUSTOMER VALUE, INC.

When the branding message of your corporation is one of high quality and responsibility, the perception of your various product brands will generally also be high. And a product perceived to be superior and representing the highest quality can command top price, on average 9 percent higher than competitors' similar products, according to a study by The Strategic Planning Institute in association with The Ogilvy Center for Research and Development.

　　Larry Light of the Coalition for Brand Equity concurs but is concerned over a trend to demarketing: "Leading brands emphasize and represent maximum quality, giving them the ability to command premium prices.

　　"Yet while leading brands remain powerful, they are being sold out. Too many marketers are emphasizing price over quality, the hallmark of any brand. Focused on short-term sales, such demarketing is reducing the equity that brands have earned with consumers over long years, and at significant cost. The net effect?

Brand loyalty is weakened. And loyalty is the aim of brand marketing.

"Wherever a market and quality brands exist, demarketers are shifting the consumer focus from quality to price, from value to volume. Service brands and business-to-business brands are being hurt right alongside packaged goods brands, store brands, and corporate brands.

"But marketers do not have to watch the decline of the top brands they created. Brands are trustmarks. When they are marketed that way, marketers can forge strong, enduring, and highly profitable bonds with customers. The loyalty that results is the basis for the enduring, profitable growth of brands."[1]

THE LENS SHOULD BE QUALITY

Quality is still the key branding message for many companies. Its central role has been reemphasized by the increased pressures on corporations from tougher global competition, the new demands from consumers, employees, shareholders and other target constituencies, and the changes brought about in the ways we communicate (and even think), according to Joan H. Walker, managing director of marketing communications for NYNEX Corporation.

"We need a new model for advertising, a new paradigm," says Ms. Walker. "And the lens for this new paradigm should be quality."

"Because quality programs have become so central for so many [companies], one needs to know the basic elements of total quality management." According to Walker, all such programs share several basic principles, including: the customer is the final arbiter of quality in all cases; work is a process based on value chains, in which all steps are measured to determine how much value they add to all stakeholders; quality improvement is a continuous cycle; and, finally, people who make quality happen create an institutional memory that reinforces the process.

To repeat (and it is worth repeating): the increased pressure on corporations—tougher global competition, new demands from shareholders, employees, consumers—as well as the media have changed how we communicate, even how we think.

One needs to know how to communicate the message of quality convincingly to all constituencies. And, often each of these constituencies defines quality in a somewhat different manner or in terms of a different set of criteria. The challenge, then, becomes one of developing and communicating a consistent, integrated message to multiple groups with corresponding multiple interests and perceptions.

Essential Characteristics

A powerful, believable corporate message is certainly invaluable to the support of a company's product brands and to the building and maintaining of a broad base of loyal customers. The specific message and communications strategy depend, of course, on your company's needs. But l suggest you consider the following points, which are generally accepted to be essential characteristics of any successful corporate branding program.

- Simplicity: The best corporate campaigns do not seek to be all things to all people. Rather, they focus on a single important idea that can be developed over time and presented in a variety of creative executions and communications techniques.

- Uniqueness: The message a company selects must differentiate it from competitors—must set it apart from the crowd.

- Appropriateness: Good corporate advertising brings attention to a company; great corporate advertising brings attention to qualities that further corporate objectives.

- Relevance: The best corporate branding campaigns hit home with their target audiences, which are usually rather narrowly defined.

- Foresight: A key objective of corporate branding is to quickly create positive impressions on target groups before they can formulate any negative opinions.

- Continuity: A successful program requires high visibility for the long term.

- Credibility: A corporate branding campaign, no matter how well planned, funded, or executed, cannot succeed if the message does not match reality.

Your single corporate brand message should be reflected in all your advertising, both corporate and product, in your direct mail, public and investor relations, employee relations, community and government relations, sales promotion, trade show participation—in any and all forms of company communications, internal as well as external.

A COSTLY ERROR IN JUDGMENT

"Quality is a more fundamental driver of competitive position and business results than any other factor," comments Bradley T. Gale. The dramatic reversal of fortune at
Schlitz Brewing illustrates what can happen when a firm
adopts the prime directive of producing its product at
least cost.

In the early 1970s, Schlitz, the second largest brewer of
beer in the United States, began a cost-cutting campaign.
Management decided to reduce the quality of the ingredi-
ents in their brew, switching to corn syrup and hop pel-
lets, and shortening the brewing cycle by 50 percent.

Although at first profit did increase, Schlitz' volume and
profit soon began to fall rapidly. By 1980, sales had
declined 40 percent. Schlitz' stock price collapsed from
$69 to $5, and finally another beer company took over the
ruined brand.[2]

A FRESH LOOK AND ATTITUDE

Superior quality is a highly desirable corporate characteristic, but it
is not the only basis for a corporate message. Nationwide Insurance
is one company that decided on another.

According to R. Steven Johnston, vice president for advertising
& promotions, "Nationwide in the early '80s took their eyes off the
ball and let the company slip into a precarious financial position.
Image and brand awareness campaigns were curtailed, while competitors continued to build their budgets and market share."[3]

In time the company got the message and started to concentrate
on rebuilding their balance sheet. By 1990, they were back on solid
financial ground and ready to grow again. Agents were clamoring
for more advertising, while customers complained about seeing
their auto premiums go up all the time with no relief in sight.

Says Johnston, "We looked at all the factors affecting the high
cost of insurance: fraud, labor costs, medical cost, safety, speeding,
DUI, and others. No single company, regardless of ad budget, could
begin to address all of these subjects sufficiently. We would have to
pick one. We chose DUI, drunken driving, and dedicated ourselves
to being the company that was doing something about it.

"Since this was not just an ad problem, we were very conscious of our efforts to fully integrate all other activities to the issue, as well.

"Alcohol detectors were donated to police, sheriffs, and troopers all over the eastern United States. Over 1,500 of them. We rely on local market publicity and limited ad support to tell this story. We have also gotten endorsements from all the major law enforcement organizations for these efforts.

"Agents went into high school driver's education classes and told teens about their responsibilities as new drivers. In Knoxville, Tennessee, this straight talk got our materials adopted by all the high schools in that market as part of their curriculum. They use our materials with our logo all over for every kid in the country, at little or no cost to us.

"Naturally, advertising plays a role," comments Johnston. "We have done some wonderfully innovative things, including a regular annual insert in USA Today just before New Year's Eve, and a very innovative TV spot, too. These materials are used throughout the year during our regular ad schedules to reinforce in viewers' minds that we're the company doing something about DUI."[4]

Nationwide's most successful program is called Prom Promise and is aimed at teens. It has had several interesting side benefits for the company. Agents go to high schools in their home towns, arrange with the administrators to run the program, and then sell it to the kids at assemblies. The kids are asked to sign a pledge not to drink and drive on prom night.

KIDS COMPETING WITH KIDS

"It's not, of course, all that simple," continues Johnston. "The key to success is to make it fun for the kids to do the program, so we put together creative competitions between schools in the area—kids competing with kids. The first two years featured rap songs or cheers that were judged by educators and media celebrities. Prizes were T-shirts for the kids, cash for the school, and PR for Nationwide. Once we had the kids, the teachers went along. In subsequent years we've scaled back the contest to scrapbooks or plans, but we've seen little drop-off in enthusiasm.

"We also went to the top teen radio station and top adult news TV station and offered them money for significant promo time, . . . as well as on-air appearances, endorsements by anchors, and so on. They also got significant portions of our spot buys. They were, in effect, our partners, the exclusive carriers of our Prom Promise messages.

"Finally, we put a PR practitioner in every major market to be sure that our agents got the local market publicity they needed to make the program a success.[5]

100 PERCENT HIGHER BRAND AWARENESS

"And it is a success," points out Johnston. "[In one year] one million teens in eighteen states signed the promise. Over 1,500 high schools and 1,300 Nationwide agents participated. We know of only one case in all of those schools where one of the students was involved in an incident, and that was the first reported to us in four years. Of equal interest, our modest $1.6 million investment in radio and TV time and PR has generated over $9 million in coverage, leading to a 100 percent higher brand awareness in Prom Promise markets than in other markets we serve.

"I can also report that our policyholders tell us that they're proud of our efforts; our awareness is up, so market share can't be far behind."[6]

PAYBACK BY DIRECT ACTION

Very often a corporate branding message leads to a specific action on the part of the customers that helps improve the bottom line. Rockwell had such an experience. Their director of corporate and community relations, commented in a recent interview:

> We are trying to create a perception of Rockwell as a high tech diversified company, not just an aerospace company. We want to communicate that we're progressive, applying a lot of new management practices to serving our customers better.
>
> We call our new theme "Leadership Performance." More than just a catch phrase, it touts the market leadership of our businesses, promoting performance qualities like innovative technology and advanced management practices. The result is a continuous improvement of customer responsiveness.
>
> The idea, of course, is to accomplish more than simply the enhancement of image. By increasing the recognition of Rockwell as the parent, we bring corporate strength to our individual brand names and help our business units sell their products as well as help us sell their stock.

*Because we are high tech and diversified, it is impor-
tant for a potential customer to understand what we
might do in one business area that could be applicable to
their own business.*

*For example, as the result of a corporate image
advertisement we ran, a railroad executive asked: "If you
can make electronics for airplanes, why can't you do it
for railroads?" That single corporate effort resulted in
generating a whole new business and profit center for us.*

WHEN TWO GIANTS GET TOGETHER

What happens when two major players in the financial world
merge? In the case of the Chemical Bank-Chase Manhattan merger,
the result was the creation of the largest bank holding company in
the United States. What kind of corporate brand would this combination of giants create? What would be their message?

According to Aubrey E. Hawes, vice president and director of
advertising and promotion at The Chase Manhattan Bank, "We
found that regardless of constituencies, at home or overseas, the
merged entity would be considered a very powerful global institution, with high name recognition and tremendous capabilities in
both commercial and retail banking. We also heard concerns, however, that we might become . . . 'impersonal,' despite the fact that
historically both institutions were very much customer focused and
relationship driven. This was an alarm of potential trouble. . . ."

The bank saw its opportunity. Because of the wide scope of
product capabilities and the depth of the talented, knowledgeable
staff, the combined organization could select the best of the best.

The focus of strategies for all "businesses" was their relationships with all constituencies. Considering the bank's global presence, its in-depth knowledge of its broad customer base and their
needs, staff brains and talent, and the wide scope of bank services
and products, the combined Chase-Chemical organization was
positioned to bring something really substantial to a relationship
with both corporate and consumer customers, bringing the power
of many resources to bear on identifying solutions to financial
problems.

To communicate this capability, the bank developed alternative
advertising executions—TV as well as print—for wholesale as well
as retail business. These ads demonstrated how the bank combined
its capabilities to provide better customer solutions. Advertising

positioned this company as a new institution, with its roots in the old Chase Manhattan, Manufacturers-Hanover, and Chemical banks and using the old name Chase Manhattan. With virtually all research with constituencies playing back the word "relationship," the bank created the tag line: "Chase: the right relationship is everything." That message is now used in all advertising and related materials.

A new logo and corporate identity system were also designed to help create a more global image, and an overbranding mechanism was adopted, placing the new logo very visibly at the top of all communications.

To stay on top of their corporate branding program, Chase conducted an initial benchmark study among 3,500 retail and wholesale customers in 60 countries (one goal being to compare themselves to major competitors) followed by a program of ongoing studies. Meanwhile, focus groups of financial analysts, CFOs, private banking customers, and employees—both in the U.S. and overseas—have been very complimentary about the merger. "It happened without any disruption in the marketplace" is a frequent comment.

When asked whether the CEO was behind the image program, Hawes replied: "The brand belongs to the CEO. We told him 'You're in charge!' And he is. Others in the company steward the brand, of course, but the CEO is fully and actively in charge. During speaking engagements, top senior officers almost always manage to work in a reference to the brand program." Smart move!

REINVENTING THE AVON WHEEL

Can one reposition a 100-year-old company? That was the question Avon Products asked themselves not so long ago. The answer, of course, was yes, but they would have to reinvent Avon to accomplish it.

"The world, it seems, was moving in Avon's direction, writes Gail Blanke, who was then Avon's senior vice president of Public Affairs. "Forces were converging in our favor. But we almost missed it. We were, as the saying goes, waiting at the airport when our ship came in.

"We were still plagued by our old assumptions, our old rules. Singing the same old song over and over sometimes dulls the ears—even of your most committed Avon do-or-die customers. What we realized we needed, internally and externally, was nothing short of a wake-up call—

a moment of self-discovery. Reinvent Avon for the '90s? It had to be done.

"What we discovered, after a year of studying trends, reevaluating our strengths and weaknesses, was this:

"We are more than just the world's largest beauty company. First and foremost, we're really the world's largest women's company. And we felt that this title carried with it a special responsibility to know more about women than anyone else, and to respond to women's needs in a way that no one else could—particularly in areas like self-fulfillment and self-esteem.

"So we recrafted our vision statement to ensure that we'd pay attention. It now reads: 'To be the company that best understands and satisfies the product, service and self-fulfillment needs of women—globally.'

"More than anything else, this vision has manifested itself throughout the company in many ways. It has helped us understand women better around the world, it has helped us to reposition ourselves for today's market, and it has helped us to become a more responsive and a more caring global company overall.

"We also feel strongly that we have a responsibility to give something back to the women around the world who have helped Avon prosper and grow. For example, the Avon Products Foundation, which is the operative arm of our Office of Corporate Responsibility, recently revised its mission to focus on the needs of women.

"We still make grants to broad areas of contribution—education, the arts, and so on. But now we concentrate on groups specifically concerned with *women's* education and *women* in the arts. By doing this, we're targeting our philanthropy to make a real difference.

"On a broader scale, we've also established the Avon Worldwide Fund for Women's Health. This program has generated major campaigns to fight breast cancer in the U.S., Great Britain, Canada, Mexico, and seven other countries around the world. [See Exhibit 5-1.]

EXHIBIT 5–1A   TARGETED PHILANTHROPY—AVON'S BREAST CANCER AWARENESS CRUSADE

COURTESY OF AVON

EXHIBIT 5–1B   TARGETED PHILANTHROPY—AVON'S BREAST CANCER AWARENESS CRUSADE

That's the number of women ... 1 in 10 ...
who will be diagnosed with breast cancer in their lifetime.

Last year, 15,700 Canadian women were told they were the 1 in 10. 5,200 died from this disease. Its mortality rate has not improved in 20 years. Its causes remain unknown.

So what does a small, golden pin have to do with finding a cure for breast cancer?

Avon Canada's Flame Pin was created to represent our fundamental commitment to women and our involvement in vital women's issues.

This year, our mission is to raise funds for Canada's newly created Breast Cancer International Centre.

The Flame Pin is only $2.00. All profits from its sale will go to the Centre. It will fund research, treatment, prevention, education, and hopefully a breakthrough.

Please ask your Avon Sales Dealer for your Flame Pin today. If you don't have a Sales Dealer, please call 1-800-665-8072 .

1.4 million Canadian women will thank you.

AVON
Let's Pin Our Hopes On A Cure.

COURTESY OF AVON

"In fact, in the U.S., we've created special breast cancer awareness lapel pins and pens that are sold by our representatives. These, in turn, have helped us raise more than $16 million to increase awareness levels of the disease and provide access for early detection.

"Around the world, Avon companies have established recognition programs to honor successful women and encourage others to follow in their footsteps. For example, in Malaysia, our Women of Distinction Awards recognize women achievers in education, business, and social work. In Mexico, Avon's Zazil Award honors women who have made outstanding contributions to society. In the Philippines, the achievements of high school and elementary school principals are recognized by Avon's Gintong Ilawan Teodora Alonso Educators Award.

"And here in the U.S., Avon's Women of Enterprise Awards have become an annual celebration of women entrepreneurs who've overcome enormous personal obstacles to start businesses on their own, and have attained significant personal and economic success.

"Our new approach has filtered down throughout our product line and into our marketing efforts. Much of it began with our 1992 advertising campaign, which spoke directly to our strength as a women's company. Today, our vision has become more than a way of doing business at Avon—it has become a way of life.

"Collectively, these efforts and others like them have helped us position Avon as a company that not only has a unique understanding of women and the issues that are shaping their lives around the world, but a company that is playing a leading role in creating better lives for the people we serve."[7]

KEEP THE PROMISE

Writes Richard A. Costello, manager of corporate marketing communications, General Electric Company, "General Electric started as the idea of Thomas Edison. He was a brilliant inventor but also a pragmatist. In fact, he once said, 'Anything that doesn't sell I don't want to invent.' That drove his philosophy and indeed our corporate culture to this day.

"His idea was to take electricity, which he saw as a fundamental driver of the economy, and build and invent things involved with the consumption of electricity—then translate that into a better standard of living. So, our promise and idea for many years was, 'Better living through electricity.' To communicate that clearly, we naturally called ourselves General Electric, because we did generally anything electric.

"An engineer in Schenectady, back in 1896, invented the logo that was put on literally every product, suggesting a system. Then, making that promise of better living, we used mass communications over many years—making fundamentally the same promise.

"For 60 or 70 years, 'Better living through electricity' was our promise. Then things changed. In 1980, about half of our net income came from electrical products. By the beginning of [the '90s] it was down to 25 percent. We needed to change our message. We started talking about better living through technology [and] emphasized more and more the trademark itself.

"Our advertising agency, BBDO, created a new theme: 'We Bring Good Things to Life.' Executionally, it was a fresh approach—but strategically it communicated the same theme we had been communicating for decades. We continue to use this theme in all our advertising today." (See Exhibit 5–2.)

Concludes Costello: "How do you create and nurture brands? (This presupposes that your company is respectable and honest and that your product or service actually delivers whatever it's attempting to promise.) These six steps reflect GE's branding strategy:

1. Pick a name.
2. Create a memorable trademark.
3. Make a promise.
4. Communicate the promise effectively.
5. Be consistent.
6. Stick with it.

"In my opinion, like GE, your brand will thrive, too, if you follow this basic strategy."[8]

LIFE AFTER MONOPOLY

We are now seeing sweeping changes in the nature and structure of the electric power industry. Regulatory proceedings and legislative activity aimed at exploring and/or promoting a transition to

EXHIBIT 5–2   GE STORYBOARD—UPDATING A TRADEMARK THEME

COURTESY OF GE

competition is now in progress in about half the states. The "point of no return" has been passed. We see a transition to competitive markets in many if not most aspects of the business of providing electric service, even in segments of the business that are likely to remain regulated monopolies.

Competition is obviously a troubling prospect for CEOs of companies that have traditionally enjoyed a regulated franchise. To see what can happen when markets are opened, utilities need only look at the erosion of AT&T's market share for domestic long-distance phone service since the breakup of the regional Bell operating companies in 1984. Since then, MCI and Sprint have grabbed about one-third of AT&T's original customer base.

While the FERC and individual states and their public utility commissions are determining how and when to introduce competition in various aspects of electric power service, utilities are scrambling to prepare for life after monopoly. There is much ado about cost-cutting, reengineering, and restructuring utility corporations for competitive markets, and so on.

There has been much less attention paid, however, to corporate branding, a concept that was not given much priority by utilities as regulated monopolies. Given the changes in the electric power industry, corporate branding should now be a vital element. A utility's image or brand can be among its most valuable assets, or it can be a great liability.

Managing the brand must become a vital component of overall corporate strategy and its implementation, especially with initiatives to:

- Position the company in new markets and reposition the company as necessary in radically changing markets.
- Strengthen customer relationships.
- Set the tone for expectations by other constituencies, such as competitors, suppliers, regulators, and the financial community.
- Mold corporate culture.
- Provide focus to an organization that will become increasingly decentralized.

Thus to compete successfully in a deregulated world, utility executives will have to build dynamic corporate brands with messages designed to leverage current equities and strengthen relationships with key constituencies. By linking the corporate name credibly and closely with such favorable attributes as quality, value, dependability, innovation, community mindedness, and good investment, corporate branding can build a special relationship with a utility's target audiences and motivate them to positive action, such as buying its stock.

Today, every organization has a corporate brand—electric utilities included. These brands have evolved over the years, reflecting decisions, business policies, and communications. Consultant Marvin Raber, formerly Vice President, Strategic Planning for General Public Utilities (GPU Services Corp.), describes the typical utility this way:

- A vertically integrated and regulated monopoly, monolithic and ponderous
- A reliable energy supplier and targeted energy advisor
- Having a public service ethos rather than a competitive business success ethos
- Serving regulators as surrogates for markets rather than serving customers
- Being risk averse, focusing on controlling regulatory risk rather than business risk
- Having minimal focus on cost control
- Having a predisposition to capital investment
- Having a collaborative Three Musketeers "one for all and all for one" approach to neighbor utilities
- Having a "softness" in business dealings; a willingness to leave more money on the table than a competitive industry participant would be inclined to do because historic regulation would likely pass excess costs on to customers with little risk to shareholders
- Being unable or unwilling to develop new businesses

Existing corporate brands may have served well in the past, but they are undoubtedly not the desired brands for tomorrow, considering the radical industry transformation now taking place. So this is a particularly critical and propitious time for electric utilities to rethink the value and viability of their corporate brands and look to creating new ones with branding messages more attuned to a competitive marketplace.

The new utility brands must promise quality, value, and company reputation. In making the transition to the restructured industry, utilities will be challenged to maintain and enhance shareholder value in the coming era of fierce competition in power markets, much tougher regulation in regulated markets, and major hurdles.

A FINAL WORD

Your company may be firmly entrenched in some well-established industry—much like Nationwide Insurance, Rockwell, The Chase-Manhattan Bank, Avon Products, or General Electric. Or it may be part of an industry in transition, an industry introducing services or products for emerging commercial markets, or an industry that is meeting new competition with a different way of conducting business and bringing its own brands into the business arena.

In any event, corporate branding offers a potential path to profitable performance. But the creation of the successful corporate brand depends completely on the message selected, and the message depends on corporate vision and values, on corporate objectives and strategy. From these you can develop and establish a uniform and cohesive message for both external and internal audiences.

Bear in mind that the selection of the audience is just as important as the choice of a corporate branding message. Some companies believe they need to reach everyone, and indeed some do. Or almost everyone. But most companies have target constituencies they aim for, and the establishment of priorities for these targets contributes much to the viability of any corporate branding program.

NOTES

1. Larry Light, *Building Brand Relationships,* Coalition for Brand Equity, 1993.
2. Bradley T. Gale, "Quality Comes First When Hatching Power Brands," *Planning Review,* July/August 1992.
3. R. Steven Johnston, "Getting More for Less in Communications," speech given at ANA Corporate Communications Conference, September 12–14, 1993.
4. Ibid.
5. Ibid.
6. Ibid.
7. Gail Blanke, "Notes on the Recent Re-Invention of the Avon Wheel," ANA/*The Advertiser,* Summer 1992.
8. Richard A. Costello, "Focus on the Brand," ANA/*The Advertiser,* Spring 1993.

CHAPTER SIX

INTEGRATING COMMUNICATIONS TO REACH CORPORATE GOALS

"I believe in integrated communications. I would hate to see a company waste resources or not fully utilize the good resources that are available."

—ROBERT A. CROOKE
VICE PRESIDENT, COMMUNICATIONS
REUTERS NEWMEDIA, INC.

The corporate world has been through so much structural change that hundreds of companies are left with seriously damaged reputations. Corporate advertising is certainly one quick way to develop or redefine a corporation's identity in order to meet the challenge of a changing marketplace.

The best intentions of corporate advertising, however, may not be good enough. The building of a company name and reputation generally requires the united support of *all* company communications. It requires corporate branding.

Corporate branding, as we have noted, combines all corporate communications programs into a single communications effort. It is total communication, internal as well as external, presenting a single, unified message—one that says clearly in one voice: "This is who we are. You can believe in our products and in our company."

It is a carefully planned and directed strategy to leverage all communications budgets together for greater efficiency and effectiveness.

From Ed MacEwen, GTE's vice president of corporate communications: "We've got to make our corporate brand campaign work as hard as possible. When it's integrated with all our other business and tactical communications, it becomes one voice—a single message mutually supporting and protecting that brand."[1]

Our Corporation Is Our Brand

Unified by a compelling vision, a company's advertising—corporate or product—can actually function as a kind of *bond* between the company and its customers. The slogan "You're in good hands with Allstate," for example, provides a common theme for all of Allstate's advertising that establishes a contract—a promise the company holds out to its customers. Not only does the "good hands" promise rally all the employees to a common purpose, it brands Allstate as the company whose employees have this mission. Terre Tuzzolino, Allstate's assistant vice president, corporate relations, describes the degree to which customers identify Allstate with this slogan. "Customers use it to compliment us when they're happy with the way we've served them, and they beat us up with it when they think that we've disappointed them."[2]

Driven by a common set of business objectives and business strategies, all of Allstate's advertising serves to "further dimensionalize" this promise, graphically and evocatively establishing the corporation itself as a meaningful brand. "People want to understand something about the companies with which they do business, the companies in which they place their trust," says Tuzzolino. Principal among the things they want to know about a company is what it stands for and what it stands behind—questions more companies need to answer in both their product and corporate advertising.

Says W. Sanford Miller, Jr., vice president and chief marketing officer for CIGNA Corporation: "Corporate advertising has to be linked directly to a company's basic operating business strategies. It should be built from a market perspective, not from a corporation's view of its world.

"At CIGNA, our corporation is our brand. Corporate advertising —or brand advertising as we call it—lets our customers and prospects know what CIGNA is, what we do, what we stand for, and what they can expect from us."[3]

The smartest marketers know that done correctly and with commitment corporate advertising works to increase market share and actually sells products. The best corporate advertising speaks with one voice, long term. It is tied to the products of the corporation, creating an environment of trust and familiarity. Conversely, good product brand advertising reflects positively on the image of the parent company.

BRAND ADVERTISING AND CORPORATE COMMUNICATIONS

Asked whether she believed brand advertising supported corporate communications, Laura Patterson, director of customer marketing and brand strategy for Motorola's Semiconductor Products Sector, responded, "What's the difference between them?

"For example," she says, "when competing products and their technical capabilities are very similar, customers often consider other factors beyond the tangible technical merits of a product. Brand building helps communicate these intangibles because, whether intentional or not, the company's brand image is a reflection of these intangibles.

"[A few years ago] Motorola's semiconductor businesses operated independently. Each organization had—and still has—individual responsibility for the design, manufacture, and marketing of their various processors, memories, and mixed-signal semiconductor products—while competing for internal resources."

As a result, Patterson said, "Few people outside of our customers' organizations, and even in them, were aware of the importance of Motorola semiconductor components within these leading companies' products. Though strategic and lucrative, the relationships between Motorola and its customers were primarily at the engineering level. Motorola wanted enhanced relationships at the marketing and executive levels.

"Today we promote the semiconductor sector and Motorola, the corporation, with our *Powered By Motorola* initiative that shows the pervasiveness of our technology. [See Exhibit 6–1.] Elements in the initiative include not only advertising, but merchandising, collateral, customer-sponsored activities, *Powered By Motorola* sponsored events, and other public communication."[4]

IT'S ABOUT COMPANIES

Peterson emphasizes: "We are not promoting just a simple semiconductor product brand. The initiative is not about chips; it's about

EXHIBIT 6–1   CUSTOMER EDUCATION MATERIALS PROMOTING "POWERED BY MOTOROLA" INITIATIVE

We are building on the skills of our **P E O P L E** and our growing portfolio of technologies to create the platforms upon which whole new *global* industries will be born.

companies—ours and our customers'. Although the advertising is business-to-business, it's not about products. It's about partnership, qualities.

"We are certainly meeting our objectives," she concludes, "to enhance relationships with key customers, to preserve, maintain, and reinforce the Company's presence, and to reinforce and influence the buy-decision. Motorola, the name and the corporation behind it, is the significant 'magic ingredient' in accomplishing these objectives."

Compare these stated marketing objectives with those cited by corporate respondents to our Corporate Advertising Practices study, sponsored by the Association of National Advertisers, Inc. Seventy-six percent answered that the primary role of corporate advertising is "to strategically position or brand the company." Provide "unified marketing support for products and services" was also offered by a majority of respondents.

Still other respondents to the study mentioned "build the reputation of the core brand through consistent messaging, supported by cohesive and coherent brand visibility throughout operations and communications." Previous studies suggested that providing "a level of awareness of the company, the nature and/or diversity of its business interests, and enhance its reputation" as the major objective.

In this sense, there seems to be little difference between the usual, accepted objectives of corporate advertising and those set by Motorola for their brand advertising.

NEW DIMENSION FOR A COMPANY'S IMAGE

Discussing the role of corporate communications, Bob O'Leary, formerly vice president of public relations and advertising for the Unisys Corporation, has stated, "I don't even want to call it corporate advertising. It's really product advertising—only Unisys is the Product."[5]

AT&T's Jim Speros, Director of Corporate Advertising and Brand Management, agrees:

> I like to call it brand advertising. To call it corporate, I believe, diminishes its role. It's really one of the sharper arrows in our quiver and helps build, enhance and leverage the equity of our brand.
>
> Brand advertising should not operate in a vacuum. It must be linked to the corporation's strategies and goals.

In doing so, it builds brand equity that includes awareness and familiarity, customer loyalty, perceived quality, and positive associations. Good brand advertising allows a company to leverage its brand equity immediately, not ten years out. If it's relevant to the consumer and offers a meaningful set of benefits, brand advertising can add a new dimension to a company's image which can be used to differentiate it from its competition.[6]

Speros manages and directs AT&T's worldwide corporate advertising program, including corporate identity, new product nomenclature, and the use of the brand by mergers and joint ventures. He knows the importance of effective brand advertising.

The company views the AT&T brand as its most precious marketing asset and a source of enormous power in the marketplace. In the AT&T view, the brand is the basis for building and maintaining trust with the consumer. It enhances the credibility of the company behind the product.

So, what's the difference between brand and corporate advertising? Very often, very little.

Adds Jim Garrity, director of marketing communications for COMPAQ Computer Corporation: "Since our corporate name is the dominant brand on all of our offerings, we find we don't have to draw a hard line between product advertising and corporate advertising. Our advertising includes a recurring set of messages that enhance the brand, and each message reinforces the others. The aggregate impact is extremely positive."[7] [See Exhibits 6–2A and B.]

WHAT'S IN A NAME: VALUATING THE ASSET

By tying the company name closely to desirable corporate characteristics such as quality, value, dependability, and innovation, corporate branding campaigns build a special relationship with all target audiences, motivating them to take wanted, constructive action. The beauty of a corporate branding campaign is that it can reach multiple audiences simultaneously, yet influence each audience differently.

"Performance is a must," says Mary Lou Kromer, former director of advertising and community relations at Rockwell. "But having a favorable corporate reputation or image can provide a significant competitive edge. And communicating through advertising helps gain that advantage."[8]

An annual *Fortune* brochure on "America's Most Admired Corporations" states: "You won't find [reputation] on the balance sheet, and it's not listed in a 10K or a proxy. If you ask the wizards on Wall Street exactly how it figures into a company's net worth, be prepared for some mighty blank stares. But more and more companies are now coming to realize that, when managed correctly, a good name can be their most valuable, enduring asset."[9]

EXHIBIT 6–2A   MUTUALLY REINFORCING ADVERTISEMENTS FOR COMPAQ

EXHIBIT 6–2B   MUTUALLY REINFORCING ADVERTISEMENTS FOR COMPAQ

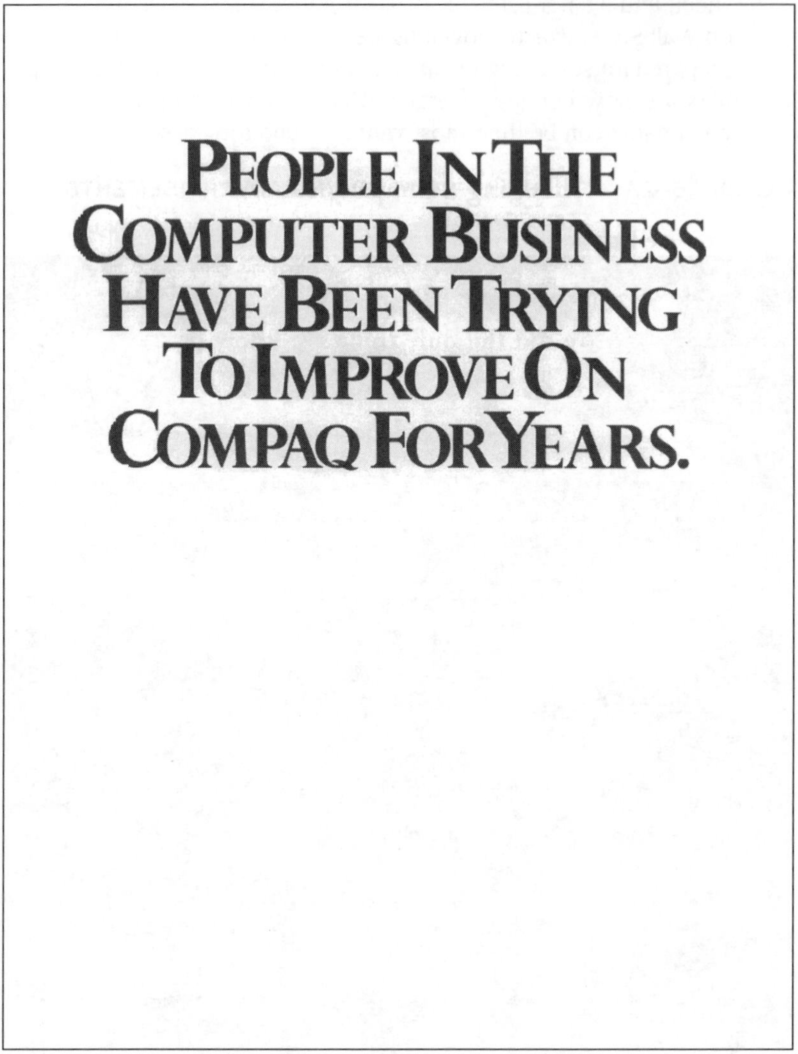

PEOPLE IN THE COMPUTER BUSINESS HAVE BEEN TRYING TO IMPROVE ON COMPAQ FOR YEARS.

It is also an asset that can prove hard to hold on to. For a number of years *Fortune* has polled leading executives and financial analysts, asking them to evaluate major corporations on the basis of eight descriptive measurements. This analysis results in a tabulation of those companies that are "most admired." Interestingly enough, of the ten companies that ranked highest in 1983, only one made the top ten in 1995. Hewlett-Packard—and it had slipped from second to tenth.

So the question is: How do you run a company when your largest asset keeps fluctuating in value?

Alexandra Ourusoff, in *Financial World,* describes the problem facing the chief executives of many companies.

> *While our third annual ranking of the world's top brand names presents companies of all types, the companies have two things in common. First, their most valuable assets are their brand names. And second, the value of those names has never been subjected to more gyrations. It used to be that if you created a brand name, you were set for life. Your company stood for quality and consistency, and perhaps even had a bit of snob appeal. Life was swell. That is no longer true.*[10]

"Knowing the value of that asset," agrees *Financial World's*[11] Geoffrey N. Smith, "and how it is changing over time, is information critical to management's ability to gauge how well its strategy is working. A company whose brand values are rising but whose earnings are falling may be investing heavily to add value to those

WHAT IS THE VALUE OF A BRAND NAME?

David A. Aaker, in his book *Managing Brand Equity,* asks the following: "What is the value of a brand name? Consider IBM, Boeing, Betty Crocker, Ford, Weight Watchers, Bud, and Wells Fargo. What would happen to those firms if they lost a brand name but retained the other assets associated with the business? What would it cost in terms of expenditures to avoid damage to their business if the name were lost? Would any expenditure be capable of avoiding an erosion, perhaps permanent, to the business?

"Black & Decker bought the GE small-appliance business for over $300 million, but only had the use of the GE name for three years. After going through the effort to change the name, their conclusion was that they might have been better off simply to enter the business without buying the GE line. The cost to switch equity from GE to Black & Decker was as high as developing a new line and establishing a new name. Clearly, the GE name was an important part of the business."[12]

brands. Conversely, a company whose earnings are rising but whose brand values are falling may well be headed for trouble."

A COVENANT BETWEEN COMPANY AND CONSUMER

Writes Larry Light of the Coalition for Brand Equity, in his *Building Brand Relationships:* "It is no coincidence that highly profitable brands dominate their markets. Quite the opposite. Dominant brands are always the profit leaders. Number One brands not only sell more product, they sell it at higher prices.

"A brand is a trustmark. A brand is a covenant between a company and the consumer, and a trusted brand is a genuine asset."[13]

It should go without saying that a quality brand has to be more than a quality product. A quality product or service must be marketed in a quality manner. Quality must be deeply involved with *every aspect of every consumer contact.* The product, its advertising and promotion, the purchase experience, product service, customer information, customer relations, and the follow-up marketing should all reflect that quality.

This is an important point to remember when building a convincing corporate brand. You need all forms of corporate communications to assure an enduring, successful reputation in the marketplace. The synergistic effect of advertising, promotion, and public relations is very powerful. They must work in concert, not in conflict, to build a profitable, dominant brand.

THE MOVE TO INTEGRATED COMMUNICATIONS

The merits of integrated communications are increasingly acknowledged by marketers these days.

In our Corporate Advertising Practices study, the majority of ANA respondents—83 percent—reported that their corporate advertising is integrated with other communications, usually through a common theme, but also through target markets, graphics, and style. Corporate advertising is most often integrated with public relations efforts, but is frequently integrated with product advertising and internal communications as well.

Integrated marketing communications has advanced well beyond attaching a common tagline to different elements in a campaign. Here's how one company, 3M, has approached it.

In a talk addressing an ANA Business-to-Business Marketing Communications Conference, Bruce Moorhouse, manager of 3M's Corporate Marketing Communications, included the following remarks:

> 3M continues to be ranked very highly in terms of America's most admired corporations. This reputation really does carry through on all of our communications, and that's what we wanted to build our communications strategy around.
>
> About two years ago we presented to management a global identity strategy for the whole corporation. That was the answer we came up with to try to solve the problem, with a five-year roll-out planned. It was really a strategy to leverage all of our communication budgets together.
>
> One of the things we wanted to do was build on the 3M personality as the foundation of the identity strategy and that what the organization is really known for is innovation. That is one of the core founding principles of the company, the major focus of the strategy in all our communications. [See Exhibits 6–3A and B.]
>
> Another part of the strategy was to link the 3M brand with our products—to link that 3M logo with all of the brands and all of our products.
>
> We think there's a tremendous advantage in leveraging off the power of the 3M brand, and we think it provides us with a framework to upgrade (and integrate) all of our communications materials around the world.[14]

YOU CANNOT SEPARATE THE SYNERGY

More companies should pay greater attention to Don E. Schultz, professor, Medill School of Journalism at Northwestern University. In discussing integrated marketing communications recently, he commented:

> Traditionally what we've done is wandered around and measured advertising over here, measured direct marketing over there, measured public relations somewhere else, measured promotion off in this area, and then said, "Well, we're really doing a fine job here. Our sales

EXHIBIT 6–3A   PRINT ADS BUILDING ON 3M'S REPUTATION FOR INNOVATION

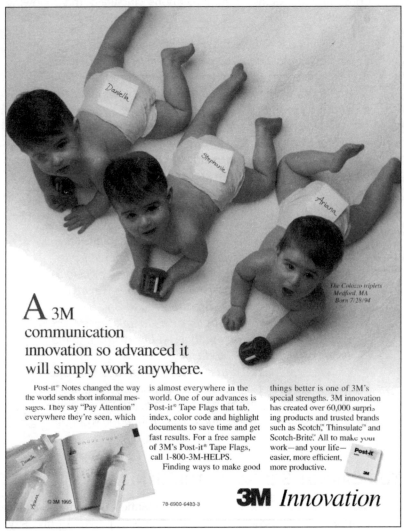

COURTESY OF 3M

promotion is really working. Our PR is really working. It's the advertising guys that are falling down."

But we've never looked at them in combination. When you start talking about integration, suddenly you can't say, "Well, the advertising is working and the PR is not working," because what you're looking at is how these communications programs all fit together.

EXHIBIT 6–3B PRINT ADS BUILDING ON 3M'S REPUTATION FOR INNOVATION

COURTESY OF 3M

I never look at the elements individually. I look at marketing activity. I group them together because I know there's synergy between advertising and direct marketing and public relations and promotion and all those other things. Quite honestly, it is silly to try to break them apart.

If they work together, why do you need to know what advertising does and what sales promotion does? You cannot separate the synergy. But you can look at them in groups of communication efforts and try to understand how they work together and why they work together and measure their impact.

Then you can say that it really doesn't matter whether advertising contributes 63.7 percent and public relations contributes 9.63 percent and so on. What we're looking at is how they together impact the marketplace.15

LIMITED ACCEPTANCE

While many companies are beginning to recognize the value of corporate branding and are beginning to appreciate how such a program can certainly achieve desired corporate goals and impact the marketplace, a number of others do not.

But if corporate branding is so effective, if it is so "right" for today's marketplace, why don't all corporations employ it? Why do such giant corporations as American Brands, Procter & Gamble, and General Foods, among others, continue to promote individual brands and product lines and ignore corporate branding power?

Why haven't they discovered that corporate branding can prove a highly effective marketing tool—one that can give a company the means to further build its name and image by communicating to their publics a single, strong and definitive message?

Reasons, of course, vary, just as the companies involved and their particular needs and goals vary. A number of these reasons are discussed in Chapter 13, "Corporate Growth versus Status Quo." But whatever individual reasons may be for ignoring the power of corporate branding, one point is abundantly clear: Old customs and traditions die hard!

NOTES

1. GTE, Ed MacEwen, ad placed in *The Wall Street Journal.*
2. Terre Tuzzolino, "Integrating in a Decentralized Environment," speech delivered to Corporate Communications Conference, sponsored by ANA (Association of National Advertisers, Inc.) September 12–14, 1993.
3. CIGNA, W. Sanford Miller, ad placed in *The Wall Street Journal.*
4. Laura T. Patterson, "Tough Business Calls For Sharper Marketing Tools," *The Advertiser,* 1994.
5. Unisys, Bob O'Leary, ad placed in *The Wall Street Journal.*
6. AT&T, Jim Speros, ad placed in *The Wall Street Journal.*

7. COMPAQ, Jim Garrity, ad placed in *The Wall Street Journal.*
8. Rockwell, Mary Lou Kromer, ad placed in *The Wall Street Journal.*
9. *Fortune* promotional brochure.
10. Alexandra Ourusoff, "Brands. What's Hot. What's Not." *Financial World,* August 2, 1994.
11. Geoffrey Smith, "What's in a Name?" *Financial World,* August 2,1994.
12. David A. Aaker, *Managing Brand Equity.* The Free Press Division of MacMillan, Inc., 1991.
13. Larry Light, *Building Brand Relationships,* Coalition for Brand Equity, 1993.
14. Bruce Moorhouse, "Success in Integrated Marketing," speech given at ANA Business-to-Business Marketing Communications Conference, April 10–12, 1994.
15. Don E. Schultz, "Gauging Impact," speech given at ANA Business-to-Business Marketing Communications Conference, April 10–12, 1994.

CHAPTER SEVEN

THE MULTIPLIER EFFECT ON KEY AUDIENCES

"Customized marketing is what we use to communicate 'appropriately.' It's sending the right message to the right person, or persons, at the right time with the right frequency, with the right offer in that message about the right product."

—W. DAVID VINING
DIRECTOR OF CUSTOMIZED MARKETING
COMPAQ COMPUTER CORPORATION

The difference between product and corporate branding is that with product branding you target one consumer or consumer segment with a single message. In corporate branding you are targeting multiple audiences with a key single message that is meaningful to all, although each constituency may regard the message differently. It's this multiplier effect that gives the corporate branding program its power.

The corporate brand message must say the right thing to the right audience at the right time. In order to accomplish this, a thorough understanding of your company's corporate brand is an absolute necessity—what it is and how it works, and why it is the most cost-effective way to improve so many aspects of your company's performance.

It is also important to realize that many forces are at work today changing the fabric of your corporate brand. These forces work constantly, some in the financial and business communities, some in government, and some within society itself. Some are on a global scale, and still others may begin at home with a single employee or customer. The cumulative effect of these forces bears directly and powerfully on your corporate brand and on the perceptions of your company held by your different target publics.

Whether you plan for it or not, the image those publics have of your company changes every day. Some of the changes are subtle, taking place over a long period of time. Some are sudden, like activism by large investors or an unforeseen crisis. Many changes are beneficial and help improve corporate brand perception by your various target publics.

JUST THE RIGHT AUDIENCE

Whatever the changes, communication is the key to promoting and managing your corporate brand. Sometimes it will be the only major competitive advantage a company will have. Thus maintaining the quality of your corporate message and aiming it at the right audiences is critical to building a strong, meaningful corporate brand.

Comments Don E. Schultz of Northwestern University: "You're in the brand business with corporate advertising just like product people are in the brand business. Today, you must build a brand for your organization. How do we build value so that people will say, 'I want Du Pont,' as opposed to a competitor? How do we build value into the brand so that people will say, 'I want a Ford,' not one of the other guys, when they're all the same? You must build corporate brands because you won't have any unique products or services. It doesn't make any difference who you are."[1]

The selection of the primary audience—or combination of audiences—depends a great deal on corporate mission and strategy. You must know who you need to talk to and have a complete database on each and every target group. This includes corporate investors, financial analysts, stockholders, as well as customers, employees, and all the other people who are involved. The only way you can ever measure ROI on communications is to know precisely who your audiences are.

KNOW WHO THEY ARE

The critical ingredient is your database. Customers and prospects, gatekeepers, investors, financial analysts, employees, the media, legislators, regulators, all the influentials should be in your database. Your corporate communications program must segment each one of these groups individually.

Not only know who they are, know *where* they are. Be able to measure what happens to them, because that's the only way to get to know what they're worth, what they do, how they respond, what it costs to get that response, and what the response is worth.

The corporate audience can be divided and organized into four major groups: business leaders, activists, the financial community, and government leaders. Of course, customers and prospects, employees and potential employees, investors, the trade, and even suppliers and the media are also highly important targets.

In completing my study on Corporate Advertising Practices for the Association of National Advertisers, a key question determined the importance of various target audiences by our respondents. The majority, 53 percent, ranked business-to-business customers first, with prospects at 45 percent. This was followed by the consuming public at 41 percent.

Other leading publics included government and the trade, each at 36 percent, and the financial community at 35 percent. Activists/opinion leaders, plant communities, employees, vendors, and "entire population" were also named frequently.

EMPLOYEES ARE A PRIMARY AUDIENCE, TOO

If customers are a key target for a corporate program, employees, too, are vital to a company's success. Just how important is evident in Doremus' work for Bankers Trust Company.

According to Phil Sievers, senior vice president and management supervisor at Doremus, the reaction from employees of their client, Bankers Trust Company, to the current advertising campaign has been "absolutely phenomenal." He adds: "The people in the bank are more excited about it than anything I have been associated with, and I have been dealing with financial institutions for 25 years.

"The bank was undergoing a new business strategy and wanted to project themselves in a different way. They wanted to be known as the preeminent managers of risk for their customers, and it was very important that everybody in the bank was on board with this strategy and associated with it.

"The bank's own employees are a very important part of the program. Naturally, customers are, too. We and the bank receive letters from all over the world requesting copies of the ads. These come from customers and executives in senior positions in business."

A UNIFIED SET OF VALUES AND A SINGLE MISSION

The value-conscious business climate of the 1990s has encouraged many companies to turn to corporate branding in order to better define their corporate personality and energize a spirit of growth. In 1987, when Transworld Corporation spun off its restaurant and foodservice units into a separate holding company—initially called TW Services and later TW Holdings—it was the largest franchisee of Hardee's and owner of Denny's, Quincy's, and El Pollo Loco restaurants, as well as Canteen, a foodservice operation.

Common ownership, however, was about the only thing that united these separate companies and their 120,000 employees. Management realized that these separate business units would flourish only if they shared a unified set of values and were guided by a single mission. To help achieve this, TW Holdings changed its name to Flagstar. A new logo, a corporate visual system and internal and external communications plans were developed to reinforce management's commitment to a unified approach in all of the company's activities.

The program was introduced to the 1,000 headquarters personnel and the other 119,000 employees throughout the country in a ceremony that clearly communicated to all Flagstar people their importance to the future of the organization. They were the number one target audience. They more than anyone else could make or break the corporate brand. The launching of this corporate identity program took place under trying circumstances as both Denny's and its parent company were beset by multiple discrimination suits at the time.

But, as Chairman Jerry Richardson said: "The kind of change we are going through requires us to be excellent communicators. Showing our employees that our future success depends on unity and a single vision for our entire company is a high priority. Using a new corporate identity to get this message across has proved to be a great way of getting this important job done."[2]

SEEKING THE "BRANDED" EMPLOYEE

The fortunes of a business may rise or fall on how well its employees compete with their counterparts in rival companies, both in how they present the product and reflect the corporate brand.

Although especially appropriate for marketing, sales, and customer service personnel, the corporate brand should be understood and promoted by everyone in the company. The "branded" employee—which in the best of all possible worlds is every employee—should leave a favorable impression on everyone who comes in contact with the firm. This means, of course, that a company's very first target audience may be, in many cases, its own people.

As Helmuth von Moltke of BASF Corporation puts it, "Anytime you do a campaign that has as its stated intention to sum up or to personify the company, one of your most important audiences has to be your own employees.

"If they embrace it, they will integrate the campaign, the campaign line, and the sense of the campaign into everything they do. They will take pride in it because basically it's a campaign to and about them."[3]

The inherent value of employee understanding and support is recognized by many successful corporations. The morning that the AT&T and NCR merger was announced, employees of both companies viewed a joint broadcast informing them of the plan. According to Steve Aaronson, vice president, international public relations, AT&T Company, "This may have been the first large scale merger in which the employees heard the news before the media did. The news went out via every internal channel possible. It marked the start of a comprehensive internal campaign to keep employees informed."[4]

American Airlines is another company placing great emphasis on the "branded" employee. Reports Ted Tedesco, vice president, corporate affairs and communications, "We have extraordinary employee communications efforts. We shifted all our 18,000 flight attendants from our operating division to our marketing division. They are trained and reminded that their job is to get that customer back in the plane, over and over again."[5]

A DIRECT LINE OF SIGHT

"[Today] there are fewer layers of management to work through," says Sanford C. Schulert, director of marketing communications, Amoco Chemical Company. "It's moving away from the control-command process. [Management] wants to have, needs to have, virtually all employees in the company understanding what the company's business is and where the company is moving, a direct line of sight, so to speak, into company strategy.

"In our company, this is a massive change. And a key element in having this change happen is communication.

"Inform. Clarify. Persuade. The employees of the company have to be on the same bandwagon, moving in the same direction. They have to be convinced that this is the right thing to do. Most importantly, they have to be integrally involved in making it happen.

"I think that the environment in American business right now is that each of us can be of service to our management in internal communication. We can help our management perform the tasks that need to be done to get the company on board and communicate these missions and visions." [See Exhibits 7–1A and B.]

PENETRATING THE CORRIDORS OF POWER

Many corporations also need to reach and influence government leaders, not only in Washington but on state and local levels as well. But it is generally the federal government that is most important to a corporation's success. Virtually everything many companies do is controlled or regulated by Washington. The federal government sets the tone either first or as a follow-on behind a lead state.

Among the many constituencies that grant corporations the "right" or franchise to do business, perhaps none is more powerful than government regulators and legislators. Without doubt, a good corporate reputation can help mightily in the corridors of power. Companies must get their corporate messages across to them, positively and convincingly.

This is sometimes easier said than done. Government can be a difficult audience to target. Power does not just reside among a handful of senior leaders and committee chairpersons. It takes time to learn the names, skills, and limitations of a fair proportion of the 100 senators, 435 House members, and 20,000 or so staff members who "are often as important or more important to the work of Congress," David S. Broder writes in *The Washington Post.* "And because the cast of characters is changed somewhat by each election, the learning process is constant."[6]

As political control of Congress shifts, the makeup and membership of committees change, the centers of power move, and it

EXHIBIT 7–1A   TEAMWORK ADVERTISEMENTS FROM AMOCO

COURTESY OF AMOCO

grows increasingly complex and confusing to know who to approach, who will listen, and who might be able to help sell your idea, program, or point of view.

EXHIBIT 7—1B   TEAMWORK ADVERTISEMENTS FROM AMOCO

COURTESY OF AMOCO

AIMING FOR TARGET NUMBER ONE

Hal Heaslip, who was with Grumman before it was acquired and became Northrop Grumman in 1994, said: "Our very existence depends on the Washington, D.C. market. Our entire target audience is some combination of the White House, the Department of Defense, Congress and their staffers, and all the people who are responsible for passing budgets and legislation."

Grumman's principal target among these groups was Congress. And frequently that meant not only the people who cast votes but their staffers as well. A great deal of critical information is read by staffers and "predigested" before being passed along to members of Congress. A staffer, likewise, is the person most likely to answer a phone to speak to a constituent.

In 1981 Grumman staved off a takeover bid in part by running an ad campaign. According to Heaslip, "We asked people to take action and call their senators. Senators' staffers called up to say that they were being inundated with phone calls in response to the ads." More recently, the company mounted a campaign to fight government cutbacks.

"Our ongoing campaign is not response oriented. Its objective is to register with those people in Washington who are important to us so we have the kinds of programs and technology that make sense in today's environment of reduced defense budget. It isn't right every time, but it's an ongoing reminder that there is one company trying realistically to direct its technology into [today's] real world."

Obviously, as Heaslip points out, there is no way you can actually speak personally to all the people in government who might bring real influence to bear for your corporate success. Intelligent corporate branding, however, can take your message through any doors you wish to enter.

When Ampex, the TV equipment manufacturing giant, wanted to make their corporate voice heard, they created a series of corporate advertisements to persuade Congress to set workable technical parameters for delivering high definition television into homes.

Says George A. Merrick, president, Ampex Recording Systems Corporation, "The purpose of the Ampex HDTV campaign was to ensure that this important issue be carefully considered despite pressure for prompt decisions. At Ampex we realized that we too must take an active role on the issue. What we supported, however, was not immediate decisions, but sufficient time to consider carefully the HDTV question and its implications on American technology leadership, international trade, and society as a whole."[7]

BECOME A MESSENGER OF CHANGE

Collectively, as well as individually, many manufacturers are recognizing the importance and value of the corporate brand. From *The*

Wall Street Journal: "After more than a decade on the defensive, American manufacturers are embarking on an aggressive campaign to win friends and influence people. Not only are they redoubling their traditional lobbying efforts among members of Congress, they are beginning to court the public at large."[8]

Their goal, of course, is to erase the image of a slow, behind-the-times, uncompetitive industry that was so deeply ingrained in the public's mind during the manufacturing trauma of the 1970s and early 1980s. Then American manufacturing seemed almost synonymous with obsolescence. American cars were out of date. Our steel was too expensive. Household products manufactured in the United States found it difficult to compete with a tide of Japanese-made videocassette recorders, televisions, and portable cassette players.

Recalling those grim days, Jerry Jasinowski, president of the National Association of Manufacturers, said: "We were completely out of the debate on ideas and public policy. We had been relegated to the past. . . . [We had to] become a messenger of change."[9]

IT'S ABOUT CONTROL

Corporate branding—like corporate advertising, employee newsletters, annual reports, and all forms of corporate communication—is actually as much about *control* as anything else.

The corporate brand helps a company control its environment by delivering just the right uncensored, unedited messages toward specific ends to predetermined target constituencies.

Says Robert F. Lauterborn, James L. Knight professor of advertising at the University of North Carolina: "Companies use [corporate branding] to control the messages investors receive, and thus manage management's ability to raise capital. Corporations with strong, favorable images find it easier and less expensive to site plants. Companies also use corporate advertising to control their ability to manage their workforce, to fend off unions, or encourage quality performance by employees.

"The corporate brand adds value to an otherwise commodity product. Avis's famous `We Try Harder' campaign both influenced employees to perform at a higher level and carved a position for the company among business renters beyond what it might have commanded on the sheer fact of its assets."[10]

Thus the role of corporate communications, as it delivers the corporate branding message, is to involve people in this control process—whatever groups of people are relevant to the company's goals—and to motivate them to desired action.

But without a thorough understanding and support of the corporate branding program by the CEO and the management team, there can be no control process, and many growth opportunities will be lost.

NOTES

1. Don E. Schultz, "ROI in Corporate Image Advertising," speech given at Corporate Communications Conference, Oak Brook, Illinois. September 12–14, 1993.
2. Lippincott and Margulies, Inc., NL, Brief Cases brochure, November 1993.
3. Helmuth von Moltke, BASF, "Measuring the Impact of Your Campaign," speech given at the Fourth Annual Corporate Image Conference, January 26–27, 1993, New York, NY.
4. Steve Aaronson, AT&T Company, "Case Study: How to Blend Two Organizations," *The Conference Board,* Report Number 1002.
5. Ted Tedesco, American Airlines, Inc., "Tactics for Improved Visibility," *The Conference Board,* Report Number 1002.
6. David S. Broder, "Behind the Front Page," excerpted in "Advertising to Reach Congress," *The Washington Post,* February 1989.
7. Corporate Advertising booklet, *Financial Times.*
8. Amanda Bennett, "Manufacturers Sing Their Own Praise in an Effort to Erase Rust-Belt Image," *The Wall Street Journal,* February 13, 1995.
9. Ibid.
10. Robert F. Lauterborn, "The Role of Corporate Advertising as an Instrument of Management Control," speech given at *Business Week* symposium, June 14, 1994, Chicago, Illinois.

IMPLEMENTING CORPORATE BRANDING

CHAPTER EIGHT

GAINING RECOGNITION FOR THE SPIN-OFF

"Innovation is the design and development of something new, as yet unknown and not in existence, which will establish a new economic configuration out of the old, known, existing elements."
    —PETER DRUCKER

Any discussion of corporate branding and its impact on financial performance would be incomplete without serious attention paid to the relatively new phenomenon known as the spin-off. Reviving a corporate brand may call for drastic action, and a spin-off of some part of the company into a new company can have drastic consequences for the spin-off and sometimes the parent as well. In fact, the '90s may well be destined to become the "Decade of the Spin-Offs."

In the decade's first few years, Union Carbide spun off to shareholders its industrial gases business as a free-standing NYSE company called Praxair. IBM's typewriter and laser printer lines became part of the Lexmark spin-off. Baxter International's home care business was spun off as a public company called Caremark, and Sears spun off its financial services units.

These are but a few of the dozens of companies that have already unbundled businesses to gain efficiency, flexibility, and a higher stock price for undervalued assets. The new, spun-off company has needs too, in particular the need to establish itself in the market as a viable entity, a worthwhile investment.

James A. Miles, a professor at the Smeal College of Business Administration at Pennsylvania State University, defines a spin-off as a "voluntary, tax-free distribution of newly traded common shares in a subsidiary to stockholders of the parent company." A recent study of 146 spin-offs over a three-year period, conducted by Miles and two other professors at Penn State, shows these newly formed companies turned in a compound average annual rate of return of nearly 25 percent, well above the performance of the market overall.

"Spinning off business units into new, publicly traded companies points the way to increased economic growth, new jobs, and rising consumer confidence," according to Carol Bruckner Coles, president and COO of Mitchell & Company, a Weston, Massachusetts, management consulting firm.

THE MOST POWERFUL WEAPON

As more and more corporations spin off subsidiaries into free-standing entities, there is an increasing need for corporate communications programs to help these fresh new faces gain recognition and respect in the marketplace. In order to realize the full potential of a spin-off strategy, CEOs must understand the importance of a strong, positive brand image in establishing a successful new company.

In a unique situation such as a spin-off, it is particularly necessary for the CEO to communicate clearly and effectively. Both parent and offspring companies must ensure that the new corporate entity communicates a stable, independent corporate image in the early stages of the spin-off.

While quick to recognize the need to meet with financial analysts and outline plans for their new publicly traded company's growth and prosperity, CEOs too often fail to capitalize on the opportunity to speak to all constituencies simultaneously through a well-planned corporate communications program.

The CEO may become so focused on the details of the spin-off that he or she forgets that communications is the most powerful weapon to start the new entity off on the right foot. The CEO may believe that corporate communications is a distraction from more pressing issues, but in reality establishing and sustaining a new independent image is the single most important factor needed to reach and influence all constituencies at the same time.

For employees a spin-off is a very confusing and potentially troublesome time; a corporate branding campaign confirms that the company is committed to continuation and success. For the financial community, corporate branding outlines the new entity's reason for being, the vision of its leadership, and reasonable expectations of financial performance.

To vendors the campaign lends a sense of stability to the new company. For the communities in which the company operates, the corporate branding campaign provides a sense that the new organization is totally committed to continuing and prospering, and thus it will generate a return commitment from the community in various forms.

PLANNING THE COMMUNICATIONS PROGRAM

A memorable and appropriate corporate name, a striking logo and attractive, compatible corporate graphics may set the stage for success. Beyond that, however, management needs to use advertising, public relations, investor relations, and employee communications to deliver desired messages effectively about the new, independent company. It is the perfect time to initiate corporate branding, and get the program off on the right foot.

Planning the communications program for a spin-off should begin well before the new corporation is out on its own. The best plan should include a corporate communications campaign for both the parent company and the new entity prior to the effective date. After all, the parent company is giving birth to a new corporation—presumably one that brings solid, established value along with it—and shareholders, employees, and other critical audiences should be reassured that the parent firm will remain viable.

SPIN-OFFS ARE DIFFERENT FROM START-UPS

Spin-Offs are quite different from start-ups because they have an established base of business, existing customers, shareholders, and employees. All too often, however, the new entity, with its management born of the parent's culture, is far too slow to realize that it is also becoming communications-independent, and therefore it is slow to communicate its own vision. This sluggishness happens at the most critical time, when it is in the public eye for the first time. The impression becomes "just a chip off the old block" rather than "here's a company to watch."

Marketing directors and heads of advertising and/or public relations agency teams assigned to help launch a spin-off need to bring these key issues to the attention of CEOs, many of whom are embarking on their first term at running a company.

A NUMBER ONE PRIORITY

At the time of a spin-off, senior management has its hands full, dealing with everything from the valuation of its stock to the office space It will occupy. The new CEO must make the communications launch of the new company an important priority.

That trusted team of corporate communications professionals that built and nurtured the parent company's image probably won't come over to the spin-off. So the CEO should assign a high priority to hand-picking an executive, probably one with a corporate communications background, to help in formulating a vision for the new company and in developing a plan to communicate that vision to all key audiences.

This person should probably have the title of Chief Communications Officer (CCO—see Chapter 15), and must work closely with the CEO to establish a communications timetable. Since it usually takes six to nine months from the time a parent company announces a spin-off until the deal is completed, CEOs should take advantage of this window by starting the communications process as early as possible.

An advertising and/or media relations agency specializing in corporate communications is essential as outside counsel and to execute the communications programs quickly and effectually.

The very first communications issue to be tackled by the new CEO is naming this new company and establishing a logo and other corporate identity items. A second step in the corporate identity development process is to examine carefully the characteristics that differentiate the spin-off from the parent company. Are there parts of the corporate heritage worth preserving as the new identity is established? Will the retention of product names, packaging designs, color schemes, and so forth help customers better relate to the new company? What are the legal issues and parameters for retaining these elements or establishing new ones?

Serious consideration of all such issues should be undertaken by a Corporate Communications Task Force.

The makeup of such a group will vary from company to company, but generally the CEO will appoint the new CCO along with heads of marketing, investor relations, and strategic planning, as well as the outside advertising agency or media relations counsel. In many cases, the Chief Financial Officer, head of Human Resources, and other senior managers may also be involved.

The task force should always have direct access to the CEO, with regular weekly meetings scheduled for progress reports.

And don't forget to allocate the necessary resources. In the rush to develop operating budgets to support the spin-off's first year in business, there seems to be a tendency to over-look the establishment of an adequate year-one corporate communications budget. The Task Force will need to push for early approval of its programs in order to assure proper funding.

In my experience with spin-offs, we have recommended (and generally received) a first year communications bud-get for the new company paid for by the parent company. Aside from the obvious economy, such a move enables and motivates the new company to begin life with a strong communications program.

THE BENEFITS OF TARGETING

An area that should be pointed out to the CEO of the new spin-off company is the need to deliver the right message to each and every constituency. This is covered in more detail in Chapter 6, but suffice it to say here that many benefits come from targeting pro-grams, whether or not there is a spin-off. *Update* cites a number of these:

- Targeting provides a framework for effective communication.
- It puts the focus on the real investors.
- It helps companies focus more on their message and explain themselves more precisely.
- Targeting sharpens executives' communication skills with investors.
- It helps measure investor relations progress and success.

- Company communicators learn more about individual investment disciplines and methods.
- Targeting helps companies influence their shareholder mix.
- It can lower the cost of the investor relations program.[1]

All target audiences will want to know about operating and financing advantages provided by a spin-off. Communications, especially to the financial community, should focus on revenue and profit projections, new product plans, market position, labor and investment changes, and management's timetable for reaching its goals. The message to customers should emphasize that the spin-off enables management to focus on its core business, produces a leaner organization, and positions the organization to respond quickly to its needs.

Employee communications should center on any improvements in compensation programs being designed to attract and retain key personnel. If top management is new to the company, employees will be interested in the background and experience of the incoming leaders.

Community relations also takes on increased importance during a spin-off. Nervous public officials need to be assured that the new company plans to stay put, will support the community tax rolls, and will employ its people.

THE "BIG BANG" CONCEPT

To obtain maximum leverage for the spin-off strategy, all of the company's communications programs should be integrated—that is to say, all guns should be fired at once and in the same direction. Public and investor relations programs should commence prior to the day that shares in the new company start trading, with corporate and trade advertising campaigns beginning no later than that day. Hold employee meetings and community events at the same time to focus maximum attention on the spin-off. This "big bang" concept will make it easier to begin a sustainable ongoing communications program.

Properly planned and executed, these communications programs can establish and maintain a positive, persuasive corporate brand that will form the leading edge of corporate strategy, positioning the new, independent organization for maximum growth and success.

NOTE

1. National Investor Relations Institute, "10 Benefits Companies Are Experiencing from Targeting Programs," *Update,* September 1992.

CHAPTER NINE

CORPORATE BRANDING ON A GLOBAL SCALE

"[In 1980], the world economy was nothing more than the sum of individual economies. Now, the integration, the cross-fertilization, the joint ventures, and the breakdown of lines of culture are creating a truly global marketplace."
—DANIEL YANKELOVICH

It is difficult for a company of almost any size not to be global today. The world has become, in effect, a single marketplace, and that fact changes how and where many companies do business.

Once confined pretty much to a few dozen consumer and luxury brands, the list of U.S. products now marketed overseas runs the gamut from soap and soft drinks, to computers and packaging, to jet engines and manufacturing equipment, and a whole lot in between.

According to *Trade & Culture,* "In 1960, only 7 percent of goods manufactured in the United States faced any foreign competition. By 1985, that figure had risen to 70 percent—a multiple of ten. Half of Procter & Gamble's sales now come from outside the United States, and travelers around the world see exactly the same television commercial for British Airways, no matter where they are."[1]

SAME BRAND, SAME ADVERTISING—EVERYWHERE

Products offered by a company may differ, but their advertising programs often share an important characteristic. The advertisers

117

involved are convinced that a single theme, used in all overseas target markets, can foster short-term sales and also contribute significantly to long-term, worldwide product identity. This is especially so when that single unified theme sells the company behind the product, in other words promotes the corporate brand to help market the product brand.

Theodore Levitt, professor emeritus at Harvard University and a noted theoretician in international marketing, commented in 1984, "The global corporation operates as if the entire world (or major regions of it) were a single entity; it sells the same things in the same way everywhere."[2]

DEVELOPMENT OF INTERNATIONAL MEDIA

The development of the unified corporate branding campaign is facilitated by the proliferation of international media, particularly satellite and cable TV networks. Such relatively recent advances in global communications not only open up ever-larger market areas, but make it possible to air the same basic commercial simultaneously in numerous parts of the world.

The Atlanta-based news network, CNN, reaches more than 184 million households in 210 countries, while MTV, the music network, estimates an audience of almost 300 million in 76 countries. Print media, too, reach out worldwide. *Reader's Digest,* for example, publishes 48 different editions in 19 languages for more than 100 million readers around the world. *Elle,* the women's magazine, now has 27 editions, each tailored to the country where it is published but with similar demographics—and thus a similar advertising audience.

The growth of international media makes it possible to aim advertising at audiences unreachable a few years ago. It also encourages many firms to utilize unified global sales pitches to promote corporate brands and/or brand images. Comments Milton Gossett, former director of the worldwide board of Saatchi & Saatchi (now Cordiant): "You [can] actually reach consumers around the world with the message that [can] get them interested in buying. No reason Procter & Gamble [has] to sell their brands just in the United States when there [are] all these consumers around the world."[3]

OLD SOAP IN A NEW CONTEXT

Like inside jokes or jargon, some advertising inevitably loses something in translation from one culture to another. A broadly based brand image, however, will sustain its appeal across cultures, particularly if the communication of that image is itself sufficiently localized. Attesting to the relative portability of Unilever's corporate advertising, for example, Harry Reid, chairman of Ogilvy & Mather Europe, the WPP Group advertising unit, answered the hypothetical question "How do you put Dove soap in the world's bathtub?" by saying, "Get a good idea. Think globally, act locally."[4]

Unilever Group television commercials featured attractive, 30-ish women—Australian, French, German, and Italian, among others—praising Dove's virtues in their own languages. These commercials were all shot in one location and end with the familiar line: "Dove contains one quarter cleansing cream." This is the same theme that Unilever has used to pitch Dove to two generations, and, making only subtle nods to cultural differences, the campaign generated fresh sales around the world.

Obviously, global or multinational advertising can pay dividends. When that advertising is buttressed by the same basic message of a corporate brand in all markets, those dividends can be truly sizable. Today, many corporations, both large and more modestly sized, appreciate the value of cohesive communications, and, utilizing worldwide media expansion, are reaching out for new and profitable markets.

BECOMING A WORLD CLASS PLAYER

CEO Donald Bainton has global plans for his reborn Continental Can Corporation, involving multinational communications and shrewd acquisition. In a recent interview he asserted, "We are going to make Continental Can one of the leading packaging companies in the world again. Our idea is to grow, [by] acquisitions, good management, and bare bones corporate cost and staff, into a significant corporation [and eventually to] about $3 billion to be world class.

"Many of our customers are now multinational. We deal with people like Lever Brothers, Colgate, Procter & Gamble, Highco, Nestle, Quaker Oats, and Mars. They're looking for suppliers—whether it be for raw materials, packages, or whatever—who have an international presence. [They need to be supplied] not only domestically, but throughout the Americas, Europe, and the Far East. That's why it's important for us to have that international presence, to grow to be a world class player."

Despite his company's relatively modest size, Bainton believes it is much easier for a smaller sized company to identify and get into new, high-growth areas than for a huge corporation, encumbered by bureaucratic systems and a propensity for reinventing the wheel.

The potential in packaging is "simply enormous," claims Bainton. Continental Can is picking out lots of niches in the market, some small but many quite large, where they can make an excellent return. It's a market that in ten years could be worth $50 to $60 billion, and Bainton estimates that they will have at least $500 million of that in plastic packaging alone.

REVIVAL OF A CORPORATE BRAND

Rather than try to resuscitate a dying corporate brand, Continental Can has chosen to breathe new life into the company by means of a carefully calibrated, acquisition-driven build-up. According to Bainton, the initial impetus for this build-up came about with the acquisition of Dixie Union, a wholly owned American Can subsidiary located in West Germany.

"Dixie Union had been losing money for five years," says Bainton, "but I saw that by getting into different market niches and making some management changes, it could be made very profitable.

"Dixie Union is in the business of flexible packaging. It makes, on the one hand, machines that can be used to pack, wrap, and seal a wide variety of different goods in vacuum-folded containers and bags. At the same time, it also turns out different types of plastic films and shrink bags which, when used on their own or with the company's machines, wrap and store everything from meats and cheeses to drugs."

Operating through a holding corporation under the Viatech name, "We started selling Dixie Union products in the United States, the Eastern Bloc, and the Far East. Very good demand persuaded us to add 30 percent to the German plant's capacity, and sales increased from $25 million in 1984 to $80 million in 1992."

This expansion toward world class size and presence continued, both in Western Europe and in the United States. Onena, primarily involved in flexible packaging, was acquired in Pamplona, Spain, as well as Ferembal, France's second largest food can manufacturer. This latter acquisition in particular gave Continental Can's strategic thrust into worldwide packaging a tremendous boost.

In 1991, Bainton bought Continental Plastic Containers, one of the original Continental Group subsidiaries. It was this purchase that precipitated the important change of the holding company's corporate name from Viatech to Continental Can Company, Inc. With that change came the revival of one of the great corporate brands, perhaps the most important step of all in the company's progress toward world class influence in the packaging industry.

FROM GLOBAL SALES TO GLOBAL MARKETING

Apple Computer, longtime international marketer, sought a unified worldwide image. A worldwide product brand, Apple decided it needed a global corporate brand as well.

As reported by Bradley Johnson in *Advertising Age:* "After years of letting international divisions largely go their own way in advertising, Apple centralized management of worldwide communications at its Cupertino, California, headquarters.

"In a parallel move, longtime Apple agency BBDO Worldwide centralized oversight of Apple's global advertising in its Los Angeles office, formerly responsible only for U.S. work. Apple management made it clear to BBDO that they wanted to have the same brand identity every place and to have the same campaigns running [worldwide] to the extent that it [made] sense.

"The changes [were] designed largely to build worldwide brand images for Apple as it diversified beyond its best known product line, the Macintosh personal computer."[5]

Formerly, Apple had given considerable power to its individual international divisions, based on the theory that the company would thereby reflect local values and customs and look more like an international company. Apple has now shifted its focus from global sales to global marketing. Formerly, they had been a sales organization selling the same goods everywhere; they are shifting now to the more complex strategy of allowing for differences in design, distribution, and promotion. At the same time they are protecting brand names used around the world and supporting them with a globally recognized corporate brand.

VISION OF A NEW WORLDWIDE HOME

Another company using its corporate brand to great advantage globally is Whirlpool. Today, it is the world's leading manufacturer and marketer of major home appliances. Whirlpool's growth from primarily a U.S. manufacturer to world leader is the result of a carefully worked out strategic direction, set in the mid 1980s and meant to create a truly global corporation and a global brand.

Says chairman and CEO David R. Whitwam, "We recognized [then] that our vision of this company's future had to change to better reflect the realities of the world if we were going to remain successful. For one thing, it was clear that the U.S. market, always brutally competitive, was maturing, and that we needed to broaden our perspective."

At that time, four manufacturers accounted for almost all major home appliance sales in the United States, a market where approximately 40 million appliances were sold annually. Unable to find substantial growth potential in the United States, Whirlpool began a systematic evaluation of opportunities—both inside and outside the appliance industry—worldwide.

Continues Whitwam, "As the standard of living continued to rise throughout the world, as trade barriers began to fall away, and as global marketing characteristics emerged, new markets were opening up and we needed to pursue opportunities to serve those markets that would increase our value to all stakeholders. Consequently, we forged a new corporate strategy which we referred to as our 'global initiative'."

"At the same time," adds Bruce Berger, vice president for corporate affairs, "there was [need for] an internal change strategy, too, one that would lead to a 'one company' frame of mind in North America and elsewhere to support our global vision and drive cross-cultural sharing and leveraging. On balance, the internal challenge has been even more difficult than the external."

With growth parameters established and study data in, the decision was made to remain focused on major home appliances, but to expand into markets not already served by Whirlpool. The goal was world leadership in the rapidly globalizing major appliance market, in which approximately 190 million appliances are sold each year.

Comments Ralph F. Hake, then Corporate Vice President for Corporate Planning and Development and now head of the North American Appliance Group: "We realized that the best way to grow this company—and create greater shareholder value—was to do what we do best, that is, manufacture and market appliances. Only on a much larger scale."

Joint ventures in Europe, Mexico, and India and increased ownership in companies in Canada and Brazil swiftly followed. Continued expansion and joint ventures have added manufacturing operations and sales facilities in China, India, Hungary, the Slovak Republic, and many other parts of the world. Perhaps Whirlpool's most significant move was, in 1989, the acquisition of a 53 percent interest in the major portion of Philips' Major Domestic Appliance (MDA) business—the well known and well positioned white goods manufacturing division of N.V. Philips' Gloeilampenfabrieken of the

Netherlands. Whirlpool purchased the remaining 47 percent interest in 1991.

CORPORATE REPUTATION THROUGH DUAL BRANDING

This joint venture with Philips was named Whirlpool International B.V. (WIBV), and the investment gave Whirlpool valuable leverage throughout the entire continent. But they were starting almost from ground zero. Nobody knew Whirlpool, and some foreign populations couldn't even pronounce the name.

Studies showed, however, that in almost all markets the name Whirlpool reflected a certain vitality and dynamism. On the other hand the Philips name was seen as old, traditional, and solid. The two names together should prove a good blend. So, in early 1990, a dual branding strategy was launched to introduce the unknown Whirlpool brand in combination with the comfortably familiar Philips name.

The dual brand was promoted both in advertising and on the product itself, and through public relations, to a 24-country market. A $100 million Europe-wide marketing and advertising approach was launched, handled by a single advertising agency and utilizing significant television, radio, print, and dealer programs.

This unusual approach to both product and corporate branding progressed so well that by 1992 Whirlpool was able to remove the Philips brand name from advertising in the U.K., the Netherlands, Austria, and Ireland. They did, however, leave the dual branding on the products until 1993. In the meantime, as single brand advertising progressed to other countries, Whirlpool was running several years ahead of projections in terms of recognition awareness and single branding. The Whirlpool corporate brand was well on its way to standing on its own two feet, requiring less and less bolstering by the Philips reputation.

HIGHER PROFITS—BIGGER MARKET SHARE

Writing in *The Wall Street Journal,* Robert L. Rose reported: "Nearly three years after completing the acquisition of the European appliance business of Philips Electronics NV, Whirlpool Corp. is posting higher profits and bigger market share in Europe, even as the overall industry experiences a recession-induced slump.

"While some companies, such as U.S. rival Maytag Corp., struggle with global strategies, Whirlpool wins raves from analysts for making its aggressive expansion work. By moving into Europe and into developing nations, Whirlpool aims to tap growth areas to complement its mature, slow-growth business in North America."

"Whirlpool's strategy is to stand out with strong pan-European brands. Research tells us that the trends, preferences and biases of consumers, country to country, are reducing as opposed to increasing," says Jeff Fettig, then vice president of marketing, Whirlpool Europe, and now president of Whirlpool Europe BV.

Andrew Haskins, an electronics analyst at London's James Capel & Co., suggests that Whirlpool connotes quality to consumers. "Philips had a strong brand name, and Whirlpool has been able to build on that quite considerably."[6]

What began in 1911 in St. Joseph, Michigan, as the Upton Machine Company, a producer of motor-driven wringer washers, is today the world's leading manufacturer and marketer of major home appliances. While still headquartered on the shores of Lake Michigan, Whirlpool manufactures products in 12 countries, markets them in more than 120, and numbers more than 50,000 employees worldwide.

THE EMERGING GLOBAL CONSUMER

Continental Can's and Whirlpool's successes abroad are emblematic of what is happening in the new global marketplace. At work, of course, is the merging of markets, the result of harmonization and deregulation by the European Community. Says Ken Wells in *The Wall Street Journal:* "The upshot is an emerging 'global consumer' whose tastes are increasingly homogenized and whetted for global products.

"'Eighteen-year-olds in Paris have more in common with eighteen-year-olds in New York than with their own parents,' says William Roedy, director of MTV Europe, whose 200 advertisers almost all run unified, English-language campaigns across its 28-nation broadcast area. 'They buy the same products, go to the same movies, listen to the same music, sip the same colas. Global advertising merely works on that premise.'"[7]

Naturally, there may be language barriers and cultural differences to contend with. There can be regulatory impediments, as well. Communications in a multicultural world is a highly complex matter, requiring constant attention and fine tuning, and it should go without saying that the complete understanding and involvement of senior management is absolutely necessary.

GLOBAL COMPANY BY TRADITIONAL MEASURES

Levi Strauss & Co. is one company that knows how to communicate in global markets. The world's largest brand name apparel manufacturer, the company has annual sales of nearly $7 billion. Robert D. Haas, chairman and CEO, is a great-great-grand nephew of the company's founder. Says Walter Roessing in a recent article: "Haas has overseen revolutionary changes in the way his company designs, manufactures, markets, and sells clothing. He and his senior leadership team have reshaped its corporate culture, streamlined its divisions, downsized its work force, and made inroads into new markets like Eastern Europe.

"Historically, this San Francisco based company has been known for its product innovation, imaginative marketing, and for treating its employees well by being sensitive to their concerns." All of which, of course, makes for a solid base for what is one of the longest-running and most successful of corporate brands.

"We are a global company by traditional measures," Haas points out. "We have employees and facilities in dozens of countries, we market internationally, and we look for new leadership talent around the world.

Levi Strauss already has globalized its manufacturing process, a feat which Haas calls a triumph over old geographic limitations. "Our company buys denim in North Carolina, ships it to France where it is sewn into jeans, launders these jeans in Belgium, and markets them in Germany using TV commercials developed in Britain."[8]

To match its international purchasing practices with its own code of ethics, Levi Strauss has cracked down on child-labor violations by enforcing International Labor Organization standards prohibiting the employment of children under fourteen. But not wishing to have a devastating economic effect on the children's families, the company worked out an arrangement with its Bangladeshi contractors who had been using child labor. If they would continue to pay wages and hire the children back when they turned fourteen, Levi Strauss would pay for their schooling, uniforms, and books. Such actions can pay back important dividends in terms of brand image and corporate reputation.

Continues Roessing: "To ensure the integrity of its jeans, Levi Strauss & Co. has been involved in a global anticounterfeiting campaign. In the last three years, it has seized nearly 2.5 million counterfeit jeans, produced primarily in Asia." Needless to say this campaign also helps ensure the continued integrity of the company's corporate brand.

It is Haas's view that, "This is a company that has had a discomfort with the status quo. We're a very restless and self-critical company. So we're constantly focusing on the things we could do better. That's one reason we've managed to sustain our market leadership for a 140-year time frame."

NEW WORDS FOR NEW TIMES

Metaphors of war and sports seem to have always permeated the discourse of business. Football, baseball, and basketball have contributed much to the language of commerce. Bill Summers, manager of corporate communications for Sea-Land Service, Inc., writing in *The New York Times*, speculates that "the major dialect" for global business will be soccer. "Soccer is a dominant sport in economic strongholds like Germany and in emerging markets like Brazil. It's the national sport of most countries in Europe, the Middle East, and the Americas. Soccer's global governing body has about as many member countries as the United Nations."[9] (Perhaps "hitting a home run" will no longer signify a business coup.)

It's too early to tell if Mr. Summers's prediction will come to pass. But the global vocabulary of business has already begun to change. Although we talk about "international" marketing and advertising, perhaps "global," "multinational," "multicultural," or even "pan-regional" are more applicable today. In particular, "transnational" is considered more appropriate by at least one leading chief executive.

In defining "transnational," Henry Wendt, chairman of the Anglo-American company SmithKline Beecham PLC, says: "The transnational [corporation] shouldn't be confused with the multinationals of the 1950s to '70s, which reproduced versions of themselves in many countries. And transnationals are not international companies that manufacture products that are more or less the same for sale in foreign countries.

"The transnational corporation has a global vision and orientation that transcend definitions of national identity. It sees the entire world as its market and customer base. With that view, it locates its research and manufacturing facilities, even its headquarters, any place in the world that makes sense in terms of serving the global market."[10]

It is global vision, of course, that makes worldwide corporate branding possible—that allows a company to break old ties when needed in order to progress in an ever-changing world. A number of multinational corporations have already had the vision to move their global headquarters or a major business unit overseas. Among these are AT&T, Du Pont, Hyundai Electronics, Siemens, Hewlett-Packard, IBM, and Cadbury Schweppes. All have their corporate brands hard at work wherever they do business.

The Coca-Cola Company, too, has recently announced a basic shift in its worldview, "by eliminating the very concept of a 'domestic' and 'international' Coca-Cola beverage business in the administrative structure of its worldwide operations," according to Glenn Collins in *The New York Times*.

"In a move that analysts said was the first for any major consumer products company, but that could be imitated, Coca-Cola downgraded its United States business to just part of one of six international business units in the company's global geographic regions.

"'The labels "international" and "domestic," which adequately described our business structure in the past, no longer apply,' said Roberto C. Goizueta, Coke's chairman and chief executive officer . . . . Randy Donaldson, a spokesman for Coca-Cola, said the new corporate structure did not reduce the importance of the company's North American business. 'We see North America as a significant success, but other areas are now put on an equal footing,' he said."[11]

A GOOD REPUTATION BREAKS DOWN PREJUDICES

As positive corporate branding can help launch a company, build its reputation, sell its product, and promote its stock in the United States, so global corporate branding works in a similar fashion. Corporation after corporation employs it now to ensure successful worldwide marketing, improve earnings, attract and motivate quality employees, and build the value of the company in general.

The Financial Times puts it this way: "Many major companies would love to have the same reputation overseas as they enjoy in their home market. After all, a good reputation alone can help to break down many of the prejudices that face foreign companies in other markets.

"[Some] years ago, would you ever have thought that the Japanese motor industry could achieve such visibility and worldwide acceptability? Of course, without the right products

Japanese manufacturers would not enjoy their current status. Product excellence has been consistently supported with corporate image-building.

"The lesson to be learned from the Japanese automobile industry is this: you cannot expect foreigners to buy your products, go into joint ventures, lend you money or work for you unless you make yourself known and respected."[12]

A question CEOs should address is: Shouldn't my company have the same reputation overseas as it has at home? Shouldn't my corporate brand be global?

NOTES

1. Lloyd Dobyns, "Selling to the World," *Trade & Culture,* 1, no. 1.
2. Ibid.
3. Ibid.
4. Ken Wells, "Global Ad Campaigns . . . Finally Pay Dividends," *The Wall Street Journal,* August 27, 1992.
5. Bradley Johnson, "Apple Wants Unified Worldwide Image," *Advertising Age,* April 12, 1993.
6. Robert L. Rose, "Whirlpool Is Expanding in Europe Despite the Slump," *The Wall Street Journal,* January 27, 1994.
7. Wells, "Global Ad Campaigns."
8. Walter Roessing, "Blue Jean Boss," *SKY,* August 1994.
9. Bill Summers, "Foreign Business: Soccer Spoken Here." *New York Times.*
10. A. J. Vogl interview with Henry Wendt, "So Big," *Across the Board,* January/February 1993.
11. Glenn Collins, "Coke Drops 'Domestic' and Goes One World," *New York Times,* January 13, 1996.
12. Corporate Advertising booklet, *The Financial Times.*

CHAPTER TEN

HOW CORPORATE BRANDING WORKS FOR THE SMALL BUSINESS

"If you want to get run over by a train, you've got to lay on the tracks. You've got to make your own opportunities."
—RICHARD JACKSON
GREAT DIVIDE GUIDING & OUTFITTERS
EAST GLACIER PARK, MONTANA

Corporate branding need not be limited to Fortune 500 companies. In fact, small companies often may have an even greater need for it. The message of the corporate brand may indeed be their most telling competitive advantage.

Take, for instance, the case of the South Salem Animal Hospital in South Salem, New York. A simple change in its outdoor decor has turned the hospital into a popular landmark and increased its business. In a recent interview, Dr. Jeffrey Hudsher offered the following: "When we bought the animal hospital ten years ago, there was only a teeny, tiny sign. The hospital had been here since 1956, on a major road, but no one had ever heard of it.

THE ONE WITH THE DOGS

"I had once seen another veterinary hospital which had an animal out front—a striking sculpture. Just beautiful. I thought that's what we really ought to do. So we shopped around and found the two dogs you see, and we put them on the lawn. That very first day people started honking, just plain enjoying it.

"Then it dawned on us that as long as the dogs were out there, we might as well dress them up. Just a little at first, and then we kind of escalated on that theme until we now change their decoration every month. It has gone over big! We've even had people referred to us because of the dogs. `Anybody who has that kind of a sense of humor would probably be a caring person.' That's the perception.

"Now when I say 'the South Salem Animal Hospital, you know, the one with the dogs,' I always get something like 'Oh, that's the greatest!' People drive by other animal hospitals to get here. They bring their guests—some from other countries—to see the dogs. Newspapers stop by here looking for a story or a photo. We've become a landmark. [See Exhibit 10–1.]

"And it's not only extremely visible, it's cost effective, too. No doubt it has helped our business. Of course we try to do a great job. We think we're really a great hospital, but those dogs have marketed us quite a bit."

A corporate branding message? Of course. Not quite the same— or as imposing—as those of Sears, CIGNA, or AT&T, perhaps, but corporate branding nonetheless. The two stone dogs, with their periodic changes of wardrobe, tell the community at large, especially potential customers, that this is an animal hospital to be remembered and trusted. One owned and staffed by warm, caring people. One to be sought out when needed.

GOING FOR IT

Expectations vary among people seeking a horseback vacation experience. For those adventurous riders looking to share trails with bear and moose in Montana, Great Divide Guiding & Outfitters offers a memorable experience. Hunting, fishing, photography, and even cattle drives are all available, with guests camping out at night to enjoy flaming mountain sunsets and the warm glow of a campfire under a star-studded sky.

A two-pronged advertising program, aimed at both hunters and riding enthusiasts, is supported by promotional brochures, direct mail, and effective PR. The result is the creation and promulgation of an image that attracts customers from across the country.

Says Richard Jackson, Great Divide's host, outfitter, and guide: "Advertising makes a big difference. We target our audiences, with separate color brochures aimed at riders and hunters. The

EXHIBIT 10–1 COSTUMED DOG SCULPTURES DISTINGUISH SOUTH SALEM ANIMAL HOSPITAL FROM COMPETITION

brochures deal with general information. Letters handle the specifics. I have also installed an 800 number for use only with the advertising, so that 1 can track the source of every lead.

"Knowing when and where to advertise is critical. Not advertising in the early years was tough. Trial and error eventually led me to the right formula. Advertising has to generate leads to be worthwhile for me. No matter how good an idea may seem, if it doesn't create leads, it doesn't get more money.

"A typical headline tells it all: 'Horseback Trips and Cattle Drives in Glacier Park Area.' And another: 'Hunt Montana—Deer, Elk, Bear.' Simple but effective, plus an 800 number. While other outfitters wait by the phone for customers, we're booked to capacity. The difference is in going for it. Marketing. And I've made sure that my logo is unique, a real eye catcher to be remembered.

"I take advantage of my opportunities. I personally called the writer from *Western Horseman Magazine* and told him what I do and where I do it. The article he put together made a huge impact on our business. After it appeared, I got a hundred calls a week, but l was ready with my brochures. And l still use reprints of it.

"To maintain the quality of our trips," Jackson concludes, "we keep the groups small. We match the people to the horses—we're not a stable or a dude ranch. And I'm the key player; I'm the guy who makes it happen the way l promise it. I have to. My name is the bottom line. In effect, my name is my brand image."

From a Garage to $4 Million in Sales

A strong, well-established corporate brand can help even a one-man, home business to grow successfully. Consider, for example, the Renosky Lure Company of Indiana, Pennsylvania.

More than twenty years ago, Joe Renosky started manufacturing fishing lures by hand in his garage. Joe had grown up poor, but loved fishing the local creeks with his homemade equipment. By the time he was a teenager he was a first class fisherman. Joe was also a successful innovator, and his home-designed and garage-manufactured lures sold well with local fishing enthusiasts. The word spread, and the reputation of his lures grew and grew.

Now he does $4 million in sales each year, with a major portion of his business coming from such leading retailers as Wal-Mart and Kmart. His garage-based manufacturing operation, with family members hand crafting each item, has been replaced by a newly expanded plant staffed by more than twenty full-time employees and employing as many as forty mentally and physically disabled men and women to assemble lures on a part-time basis.

His secret of success? He has more than one, but they add up to a solid, highly credible brand. Writes Rollene Saal, "Trust—both building it and keeping it—is the sturdy foundation of Renosky's business philosophy. It's a factor when dealing with customers, as well as with suppliers and lenders.

"Everyone who deals with retailers knows that shelf space is all-important', Renosky says. `The buyer, whether from a small tackle shop or Wal-Mart, has to trust you enough to hand over some of that valuable area.'"[1]

How does Joe Renosky spread the word about his new products? He points to four basic rules:

1. "Give products away to people who can promote them. Industry writers, for example, may use the items and then write about them.
2. "Contact the pros in your industry and let them know you have something new.
3. "Take advantage of trade shows. Walk around the floor and talk to people. Let them know what you're working on.
4. "Advertise on local TV. It's not too expensive and it adds credibility.

Describing Renosky's instincts for sales and marketing, Saal adds: "His company has relationships with such high-profile fishermen as Guido Hibdon, a two-time Angler of the Year. 'Pros like that give a lot of credibility to the product,' says Renosky, 'and l get ideas for new items because they're constantly out there testing.'"[2]

Having expanded into the fishing line business, Renosky competed with a number of other companies to get the product into Wal-Mart. His ultralight Lynch Line was one of those chosen. "The buyer trusted me," declares Renosky. "Once again, the little guy is a winner." And once again, the little guy was smart enough to build a strong corporate brand, one that customers believe in and trust.

POWER IN THE BRAND NAME

Corporate reputations can sometimes be regained as well as created, as in the case of the Gibson Guitar Corporation. Gibson's history has been as volatile as that of the music industry itself. Gibson became well known for designing and producing classic electric guitars for such stars as Les Paul, B. B. King and Jimi Hendrix. With the advent of folk music in the 1960s, the coming of the Beatles, and the proliferation of rock groups, the company's fortunes soared, reaching a sales peak in 1972.

But guitar sales began to decline. And under the guidance of new management based in Ecuador that had had no prior experience in musical instruments, Gibson made a number of serious mistakes.

"By all accounts," writes Bryan Miller of *The New York Times,* "Gibson let its quality slip [with moves] that led to all kinds of stupid design changes." By 1986, the company was nearly out of business. It was then that two rock-and-roll era executives, Henry Juszkiewicz and David Berryman, seeing latent power in the Gibson brand name, took over the company.

"Realizing that Gibson's strength was in its heritage," continues Miller, "the partners began retooling the factory to recreate and improve its classic guitars, and offer a line of special reissue models of famous Gibsons of the 50s and 60s."

The partners understood that superior quality is the most basic driver of competitive positioning. Putting the principle into practice, "they upgraded every part of the operation, from wood and electronics to paint. Old sound pickups were dismantled, studied and replicated to achieve 1950s and 1960s sound.

"The market responded enthusiastically. 'Gibson is now doing everything right, and we're definitely selling more of them,' said Scott Black, sales manager of the Guitar Center in Los Angeles, the largest guitar retailer in the country."

Juszkiewicz and Berryman have taken full advantage of a powerful corporate reputation to move their company down the road to new growth and profits. To further build the corporate brand, they have publicized the pantheon of performers who play on their instruments—such artists as Les Paul, Chet Atkins, B. B. King, Herb Ellis, Jimmy Page, Larry Carlton, Slash of Guns 'N Roses, Hootie and the Blowfish, Joe Walsh and Don Felder of the Eagles, Steve Perry of Aerosmith, Lita Ford, Peter Frampton, and Dave Matthews. Rescued from the musical scrap-heap, Gibson now has set itself the goal of becoming "the largest instrument company in the United States."[3] (See Exhibit 10–2.)

TYING THE COMPANY TO A SPECIAL CAUSE

For a small company, especially one competing against corporate giants with deep pockets, a corporate branding program can be crucial. Because of their limited size and funds, it is especially necessary for them to project a novel and memorable brand. Perhaps this is why so many of them today look to cause marketing to help establish a viable corporate brand.

**EXHIBIT 10–2A CELEBRITY ENDORSERS HELP CONFIRM
GIBSON'S RETURN TO FORM**

COURTESY OF GIBSON

The strategy of cause marketing is covered more thoroughly in Chapter 11. A significant percentage of the firms that subscribe to it are more modestly sized companies that portray themselves as being socially committed. Among them is a shoe company, Kenneth Cole Productions. Says its president, Kenneth D. Cole, "People feel good supporting people who believe in the same things they do." His company has been involved in cause marketing since 1985 when they ran an ad promoting AIDS research.

**EXHIBIT 10–2B CELEBRITY ENDORSERS HELP CONFIRM
GIBSON'S RETURN TO FORM**

Large and small companies may differ in many ways. Size and funding are only the beginning. But whatever the differences, they both share in a vital need for the competitive power of a corporate brand. As much as AT&T or IBM, the little company needs to tell its marketplace "who we are" and "what we believe," and requires the same sort of sophisticated communications program to create a desired impression on the target audience.

Those smaller companies that are publicly held have a special opportunity to influence stock price. "That opportunity is the lack of investor knowledge of smaller companies that can enable them to influence positively their share valuation through effective communications," says Michael Seely, president of Investor Access Corporation. "IR people can do more for smaller companies than bigger companies," he suggests.[4]

"The company that is under-followed and under-owned by institutions will provide the greater opportunity to use communications in influencing stock price," adds J. Desmond Towey, president of Cameron Towey & Associates, Inc.[5]

Thus for the little independent company as well as the huge Fortune 500 member, corporate branding can be a valuable investment in the future. An integrated strategy that sets communications standards and policies across all units of the company will work for the corporate good by trumpeting the message: "You can believe in our company and in our products."

NOTES

1. Rollene Saal, "Hooking the Big One," *Your Company,* Spring 1994.
2. Ibid.
3. Bryan Miller, "Saving Gibson Guitars from the Musical Scrap Heap," *New York Times,* March 13, 1994.
4. National Investor Relations Institute, "Smaller Companies Have Greater Opportunity to Influence Stock Price," *Update,* December 1989.
5. Ibid.

CHAPTER ELEVEN

ADVOCACY AND CAUSE MARKETING

"We've learned from insiders at the White House that [the] President reads for himself. He doesn't rely on daily news summaries prepared by his staff. This has dramatic implications for advocacy groups. You can talk directly [to the President] using, for example, an ad in The Washington Post. *This means that public interest organizations have a direct pipeline to the President—without any filters—so that he can see for himself what people have to say."*

 —HERBERT C. GUNTHER
  PUBLIC MEDIA CENTER

We have seen in previous chapters the importance to corporate branding of establishing just the right message to reach your company's target audiences—a message that says quickly and persuasively that "You can believe in our company and in our products."

But sometimes the message isn't about the company or one of its products or services. Sometimes the message is about a critical public issue, one the company or organization may have a stake in. This is called advocacy or cause marketing.

The key audience for such a message might be the general public, but it's more likely to be targeted groups of decision makers who can bring economic or political power to bear on resolving the issue to the satisfaction of the advertiser. Groups like the government, for example. Or business leaders, or activists.

In remarks to the Philadelphia chapter of the Public Relations Society of America, Marc Rosenberg of *The Washington Post* said:

"Advocacy advertising can be a very powerful, effective tool. So, I am constantly amazed by the reluctance of some public relations practitioners to use it."

WORTH MANY TIMES THE COST

Rosenberg goes on: ". . . I suspect it often comes down to the issue of 'earned' media versus 'paid' media. For some who were trained in the old school of PR, to resort to paid media seems to be an admission of failure. It shouldn't be. Increasingly, we see that advertisements can actually become focal points in an earned media campaign."

In a study of cause advertising's role in the recent health care reform debate, Kathleen Hall Jamison, the Annenberg School's dean, documented that a number of different ad campaigns generated news coverage worth many times the cost of the ad placements themselves.

The health care debate provided a perfect subject for advocacy advertising according to Rosenberg, because the debate was so complex, so pervasive, and so prolonged that traditional public relations techniques were not adequate and had to yield to paid media. There were simply too many competing voices, too many nuances to the subject, and too long a life to the issue for interest groups to trust that traditional PR would allow their messages to cut through the clutter, be heard, and be remembered.

"Advocacy advertising provides three critical advantages: certainty, consistency, and impact," adds Rosenberg. "With paid media, you have absolute control over when and how your message reaches the public. Done properly, your ads will be an unavoidable part of the information stream and can themselves make news. And an ad campaign can keep your message in front of the public long after the novelty value of your news story has faded."

UNDERSTANDING YOUR MARKETS

There is no doubt that cause marketing works and can increase sales and profits. Cause marketing, once linked exclusively with issues of social responsibility, is now viewed as a tool of mass marketing. Understanding your markets is the key to crafting a sincere message that becomes part of the fabric of the corporate brand.

Although certainly market driven, Ben & Jerry's Homemade Inc. is not a mass marketer. They are, however, socially committed. For every cause which they support, the company has a product or flavor. Rainforest Crunch benefits rain forest preservation, Peace Pops' sales benefit pacifist groups, and Wild Maine Blueberry aids that state's blueberry-growing Passamaquoddy Indians.

There are many more examples of savvy mainstream marketers utilizing cause marketing to forge a corporate brand, although some are more successful than others. Meredith Corporation created the Better Homes Foundation through which Sara Lee's Hanes unit donates cash and clothing to homeless families. Heublein successfully introduced a vodka by sponsoring an AIDS "danceathon," organized by the Gay Men's Health Crisis.

By relating product pitches to issues of real concern, cause marketing appeals especially to those who disdain the hype and hoopla of conventional advertising. Companies so involved not only make their opinions known in their advertising, but also on their packaging, on aisle displays, on cash register signs and other points of purchase, leading to the terminology "point-of-purchase politics." For the millions of Americans who consider themselves socially conscious, point-of-purchase politics can distinguish a company as effectively as a slogan or logo.

One of the better potential cause marketing concepts is Avon's Breast Cancer Awareness Campaign. Obviously Avon is a company that understands its markets and communicates a sincere corporate branding message to them. If Avon is consistent in maintaining the message over a long period of time they will benefit by having a higher level of corporate brand reputation among all their key target markets. This not only includes their customers and representatives but also their stockholders and financial analysts.

Like any other form of marketing strategy, however, cause marketing may not always work out exactly as planned. There are risks involved. Sears, for example, promised in their catalog to donate to the Humane Society a portion of the proceeds from the sales of some stuffed animals. Certainly a worthy cause. Unhappily, the National Rifle Association complained, feeling the promotion was not in their better interests. Sears felt the pressure and stopped selling the animal, rather than risk offending a large segment of potential customers.

SLOWING DOWN THE TRUCK LOBBY

Advertising is also used to influence those governmental decisions and actions important to an organization's future. For example, in 1991, a railroad industry-funded advertising campaign stalled efforts on the part of the American Trucking Association to ease weight and size limits. Writes Don Phillips in *The Washington Post:* "Remember the TV ad that shows a mother and her two children on a highway as a triple-trailer truck bears down from behind, filling the rear-view mirror with its giant headlights and grill? The mother's face grows more tense, and then the truck passes the overwhelmed auto.

"It worked. The ad, part of a campaign that played on motorists' fear of big trucks, was sponsored by the railroad industry. It helped put the brakes on a trucking industry effort to loosen restrictions on the states so they could allow heavier and longer trucks. Dan Lang, vice president of the Association of American Railroads, said of the response generated by the ad campaign, 'We got tens of thousands of calls for more information.'

"Lang said that the commercial was intended to be dramatic. But the truck driver in it was not speeding, did not tailgate, followed the rules for safe passing, and was told specifically not to let the trailers sway about the road. 'It's like a Rorschach test,' Lang said. 'People take away from it what they see in It.'"[1]

The railroad's victory was sealed when the Senate passed a highway-mass transit bill containing a provision that would keep truck weight restrictions at existing levels and effectively prevent any expansion of routes open to double- and triple-trailer combinations.

Clearly, corporate branding as utilized by cause marketing is a powerful tool, one that can influence effectively the highest levels of the United States government.

Orchestrating Public Opinion

Advertising to influence public opinion was used most effectively to change plans of the Walt Disney Company to construct a major theme park in an area of northern Virginia where residents, among others, objected strongly. It happened this way.

At one time, the Walt Disney Company announced plans to build a $650 million theme park, called Disney's America, on a 3,000-acre tract in the little northern Virginia town of Haymarket. The theme of the park, which would cover 400 acres, was to be devoted to American history.

The plan included almost 2 million square feet of commercial space, more than 2,200 housing units, 1,300 hotel rooms, a 280-acre campground, a 37-acre water park, and two golf courses. It was an impressive plan, but all at once a lot of people decided they didn't want it.

In the first place they feared such a park would despoil the Civil War battlefield of Manassas—also known as Bull Run—only four miles away, as well as draw visitors away from such other nearby historical sites as Mount Vernon. A study by the Piedmont Environmental Council (PEC) concluded that the proposed site was the wrong one, that there were others better situated to accommodate Disney's America and the development that would surely follow.

Writes Charles W. Bailey in the *Washington Monthly*, "Despite this, it seemed highly unlikely that the park could be stopped at the local or state level. Virginia Governor George Allen was all-out for Disney: When the company asked the state to spend $163 million to improve highways around the Haymarket site, Allen went along cheerfully. Disney staged a lobbying blitz— it reportedly spent more than $400,000 in Richmond—and the legislature approved the full amount."[2]

It was a foregone conclusion that Disney would get the rezoning and other approvals needed from local, county, and state bodies. It seemed the promise of new payrolls and higher tax collections was just too much to resist. The federal government, it was concluded, couldn't be counted on to block the project, given Disney's individual and PAC contributions to candidates and political committees amounting to more than $1 million.

Park opponents recognized that opposition would have to be stirred at the national level. In order to do so, however, they would have to broaden their appeal to issues that went beyond the seemingly local nature of arguments about heavier traffic and so forth.

LOCATION, LOCATION, LOCATION

Opponents decided to go national with a single, simple argument: Disney's America was being built in the wrong place. Richard Moe, president of the National Trust for Historic Preservation, summed up the strategy with the old real estate maxim: "Location, location, location." This turned out to be a good strategy. Disney was trying to turn the debate into a freedom of speech issue—an approach designed to disarm a controversy about the proposed content of the historical park.

"The counterattack on Disney began," says Bailey, "with the National Trust taking out a full-page advertisement in *The Washington Post*. 'Please reconsider the location of Disney's America.' It included a return coupon; over 4,200 coupons came back—an encouraging response. A few days later, 'Protect Historic America' was born." (See Exhibit 11–1.)

EXHIBIT 11–1 OPEN LETTER TO THE WALT DISNEY COMPANY FROM THE NATIONAL TRUST FOR HISTORIC PRESERVATION

National Trust for Historic Preservation

Mr. Michael Eisner
Chairman, President and Chief Executive Officer
The Walt Disney Company
Burbank, California 91521-1010

Dear Mr. Eisner:

Please reconsider the location of Disney's America.

The economic debate over your proposed theme park in Virginia—whether it will really generate the state and county taxes, jobs and economic growth the company projects—will linger long past the completion of the project. But there is no debating the fact that Disney's America, and the development that will inevitably ripple from it, will destroy one of the most historic and beautiful landscapes in the country.

Disney's America, sadly, will become yet another example of sprawl. It will stand as a superscaled specimen of the leapfrog development that, year after year and acre after acre, erases the American countryside—sapping the vitality from existing cities and towns, fueling automobile dependency and its devastating impact on the region's air quality, and luring economic and social resources far away from where they are most needed.

How can this be? Disney's reputation is one of creativity and quality, not destruction. Disney's products are brilliantly conceived and expertly marketed, and the Disney brand has become a respected corporate symbol of which Americans are justifiably proud. But by leaping into a pristine region Disney joins the company of others who profit at the expense of open space and history, leaving behind a long trail of ruination at the edge of virtually every community in America. Look around you.

The Haymarket, Virginia, area deserves better. Like countless regions nationwide, this historic gateway to the Shenandoah Valley deserves nothing less than the prudent use and full protection of its abundant natural and human history. For hundreds of years residents and landowners—including the four presidents who have made their homes nearby—have meticulously tended its Piedmont forests, hamlets, farmland and waterways. See for yourself. Crisscross the area on its roads, which are prized as some of the most scenic in the country. There you will discover the real theme park—13 historic towns, 16 Civil War battlefields and 17 historic districts within an hour's drive—the themes of which are tradition, beauty and pride.

Recent studies have revealed that there are a number of other locations in northern Virginia large enough for the park that are closer to existing development, more handy to labor pools and serviced more efficiently and comprehensively by existing roads and mass transit. Certain of these sites are situated more directly in the stream of tourist traffic. You can have it both ways. If there is a market for Disney's America, the market will be there also. Developing there will bring you closer also to responsibility—and farther from the destruction of a unique historic environment.

The choice is yours. You can sully the landscape as well as the prestige of an American corporate and entertainment legend, or you can move on to a production that all of us could applaud.

Sincerely,

Richard Moe
President
National Trust for Historic Preservation

Henry A. Jordan, M.D.
Chairman
National Trust for Historic Preservation

The following organizations join the National Trust in support of this message:

Alliance for Historic Landscape Preservation
America the Beautiful Fund
Arlington Heritage Alliance, Inc.
Chesapeake Bay Foundation
Countryside Institute
Izaak Walton League of America
National Alliance of Preservation Commissions
National Alliance of Statewide Preservation Organizations
National Audubon Society
National Council for Preservation Education
National Council of Preservation Executives
National Growth Management Leadership Project
National Parks and Conservation Association
Natural Resources Defense Council
Piedmont Environmental Council
Preservation Action
Preservation Alliance of Virginia
Scenic America
Sierra Club
Sierra Club Legal Defense Fund, Inc
Society for American Archaeology
Society for Historical Archaeology
Waterford Foundation
The Wilderness Society

Join the effort to protect the Haymarket area by filling out this ballot and sending it today. The National Trust will forward your statement to The Walt Disney Company.

☐ I want to go on record in urging Disney not to locate its theme park in the Haymarket area.

☐ I would also like to receive more information on what I can do to protect the Haymarket area.

Send to: National Trust for Historic Preservation
1785 Massachusetts Avenue, N.W.
Dept. C
Washington, D.C. 20036

COURTESY OF THE NATIONAL TRUST FOR HISTORIC PRESERVATION

In addition to Moe, the original committee of opposition had included Julian Scheer, former PR chief for the U.S. space program; Nick Kotz, a Pulitzer Prize–winning journalist and author; and Peter Hannaford, image maker for Ronald Reagan. Now other influentials joined the ranks. David McCullough, biographer of Harry Truman and host of PBS' "The American Experience," agreed to help as did Arthur Schlesinger, Jr., Tom Wicker, C. Vann Woodward, James McPherson, Shelby Foote, Professor Brown Morton, and more than 200 other historians and writers.

THE MULTIPLIER EFFECT

A press conference launching Protect Historic America had a multiplier effect. Articles spurred more articles, which were circulated to encourage still more, and so on. The group compiled folders of clippings and lists of distinguished supporters and mailed them to editorial writers across the country. It was a natural subject for busy local writers. Here was a fun subject, with national implications, easily packaged, with sexy intellectual names—and all the research for the editorial was already done; no need for reporting or phone calls. (Disney's response was underwhelming: The company said it would give $100,000 to the Association for the Preservation of Civil War Battle Sites.) Thus was born a barrage of anti-Disney publicity in papers all over the country.

With the PR battle engaged nationally, public opinion was soon aroused. Opponents to the park now turned their attention to persuading federal agencies to insist on a detailed—and thus time consuming—federal study. Another member of the anti-Disney team, Harry McPherson (no relation to the historian), had impeccable political credentials. A lawyer and former White House counsel to Lyndon Johnson, McPherson had that most valuable of Washington assets: access to high officials. He began contacting key members of Congress and the Cabinet, asking for a special hearing. This eventually resulted in a congressional resolution proposed by 16 House members urging federal officials to make sure Disney was in full compliance with environmental laws.

Adds Bailey: "It was becoming clear that the fight over the northern Virginia project would be long, litigious, expensive, and messy. Dick Moe had kept in touch with people on the other side—including John F. Cooke, chief executive of the Disney Channel. Moe initiated a series of private conversations with Cooke and tried to make the case that this was the wrong location.

"'It seemed clear that they were trying to find a way out and had become persuaded that the [Haymarket] site was wrong,' Moe recalls." [It did not take very long for the Walt Disney Company to say] "it would 'seek a new site' for its theme park, explicitly [surrendering] to the strategy of the opponents: 'We recognize that there are those who have been concerned about the possible impact of our park on historic sites in this unique area, and we have always tried to be sensitive to this issue.'"

A PATTERN OF DISCRIMINATION

Advocacy can de played out on a global scale, too. From *The Washington Post:* "[Beginning in the fall of 1994], the Church of Scientology presented a weekly series of full-page advertisements that seek to focus attention on what the Scientologists believe is a pattern of deliberate acts of discrimination against them by government officials in Germany.

"Each ad represents a number of well-documented cases with specific names, places and dates. And each ad makes the point that the Nazis first started with similar, seemingly small acts of intolerance against religious minorities. Most of the ads are dominated by historical photos from the Nazi era.

"The Scientologists say they are running these ads to force the German government to address their complaints . . . and they are quite pleased with the results of their campaign which delivers their message clearly, repeatedly, and with considerable impact."[3]

According to Sylvia Stanard, a spokeswoman for the Church of Scientology, "We're going to keep running the ads until the German government is willing to realize that there's a problem. We're trying to say: 'Wake up and smell the coffee.'"[4]

A FUTURE BASED ON FAIR DECISIONS

Mobil, United Technologies, Shell, W. R. Grace & Co., and International Paper are but a very few of the more prominent examples of major corporations that have turned to advocacy advertising to advance some particular cause or message, either in their own behalf or that of the general public. ARCO is another. (See Exhibit 11–2.)

In an interview Ken Dickerson of ARCO describes their use of cause marketing to affect legislation of importance to the corporation. "Like many companies," he said, "we do not do a lot of corporate advertising. But when there's an issue we feel needs to be addressed, or when there's a story that needs to be told about our goals that has not been picked up by normal media, then we run advertising.

EXHIBIT 11–2A ADVOCACY ADVERTISEMENTS FOR ARCO

1,310,822 PEOPLE HELPED WRITE THIS ARTICLE.

ARCO customers, driving with our Emission Control Gasolines, have helped to make 1990 the cleanest year for air quality in forty years.

In fact, they've eliminated over 90 million pounds of air pollution in just over a year's time.

But they're not alone.

People are using public transportation.

People are carpooling. Businesses are doing their share. We're all doing something to reduce smog in the Los Angeles Basin.

And it's paying off — for everybody.

The South Coast Air Quality Management District reported a dramatic drop this year in expected smog levels. It's a sure sign that we can all make an impact.

Let's keep it up. Let's keep cleaning the air.

ARCO

SEARCHING FOR CLEAN AIR SOLUTIONS

EXHIBIT 11–2B ADVOCACY ADVERTISEMENTS FOR ARCO

COURTESY OF ARCO

"Virtually everything we do is controlled or regulated by Washington or by the various state governments where we do business. So, we employ corporate advertising in an effort to influence government legislation or regulation, either at the state or federal level, or to deliver a message to the public which we believe has not been widely distributed.

"If we do not communicate the message through the media to all the people that need to know, then we have to deliver it personally. That's impossible to do. There are literally thousands of people [who may have] considerable influence. So if we take a blanket approach and communicate [through advertising] to everyone that is a reader of such a publication as *The Washington Post,* the odds are we have hit the right targets even though we may not know it.

"We are an oil and gas company. This means, of course, we have to explore for oil and gas, and, having found it, we have to develop it and sell it at a reasonable price that will justify the investment and risk we are taking. Anywhere along that chain, the denial of access, price controls, or even product controls can preclude us from realizing a fair return on our investment and thus may determine whether we may or may not continue in business in the United States. Our entire future is based upon fair decisions coming out of governmental officials.

"In the past twenty years, government has become increasingly involved in our business. There has been on average one major piece of new legislation or renewal of legislation every year.

COMMUNICATION IN A HURRY

"For example, the Clean Air Act, as initially proposed, would have in essence provided that only alternative fuels could be considered as the fuels of the future. That legislation did not recognize the possibility that gasoline could be changed sufficiently to qualify as a clean fuel. This was not an oversight on the part of the regulators. It was the fact that we had not communicated to them that, under proper circumstances, you could radically change the formulation of gasoline.

"Once we saw there was a national will to develop and pay for cleaner fuels, we assigned our scientists to projects of [creating] gasolines that would burn as clean as any alternatives then being considered. Having determined that it could be done, we had to get the message to the people who were writing the legislation.

"We decided to buy space in *The Washington Post* to communicate to all of Washington that gasoline could be reformulated, that it could be made cleaner. But we had to communicate in a hurry, because Congress was about to act in a matter of days. And the only way to get the message across to the members of Congress (and all their aides, assistants, and consultants) was to publish it as widely as possible.

MEMBERS OF CONGRESS HESITATED

"It was important, too, for us to integrate our efforts—our lobbying efforts, research efforts, advertising efforts—and all at the right time. If you're going to do advertising in the area of public policy, then you have to coordinate [your various marketing communications and research]. Surveys showed us that the public wanted cleaner fuels, so it became fairly easy to make appropriate decisions. Congress was going to enact legislation that required cleaner fuels, and if we wanted to be a participant, we had to do the research.

"We not only had to do the research that would lead to the development of cleaner fuels, but we had to tell the people that we'd been able to do it, and we had to invite the government to participate with us in every step. We had to say: 'This is what we have determined. You're invited to come and look at what we have done. You're invited to test it, use it, and if you agree, perhaps you will say that [this company] represented that this product is good and we agree. It does what they say it does.'

"The outcome was very favorable. In the Clean Air Act, reformulated gasoline was one of the alternative fuels that was listed.

"Could it have been done without the advertising? I don't know. But we do know that the advertising caused members of Congress to pause in the midst of a committee hearing and say: 'What about this reformulated gasoline I've just read about? What's all that about? Is there any substance, any merit to that?'

"Then there was a moment of hesitation when members of Congress said: 'Let's look into that. If there's any merit to it we can include it as one of the listed items to be considered for the future. If it can be done without a change in the infrastructure, then it will be the least costly way for the consumer to get cleaner fuels and better air.' So the advertising caused Congress to begin to ask questions, which is the most we can hope for."

GREEN MARKETING AND TRUE CORPORATE IMAGE

Are the days of so-called Green Marketing growing shorter? Are the "green" claims by corporations becoming less and less credible? Are some advertisers merely blowing smoke to cash in on a trend?

Says one expert, Jonathon S. Baskin, corporate manager for public affairs, Nissan North America, Inc., "The environmental realities of the '90s will quickly put most corporations' environmental claims into perspective. No amount of office paper recycling or environmental citizenship will satisfactorily address macro-issues like global warming and resource depletion, and customers know it. Corporations will be obligated to do more than just market to green interests.

"The ultimate goal of green marketing will be its demise as an independent function. At some point in the near future, green marketing will be synonymous with 'smart' marketing. It will become an important but inseparable part of the overall corporate identity we promote to our publics.

"The companies that survive the death of green marketing will be those that have seen beyond marketing to communicating the real identity of the corporation. From that perspective there is no green marketing separate from green business strategy or, in its totality, any E-action separate from action on any other issue of importance to the company or its customers."[5]

It seems that green marketing is likely to survive in the long run, but only as part of a total corporate branding program.

THE IMPACT OF SOCIAL RESPONSIBILITY

Whether the target for your advocacy campaign is the government, your own employees, activists, investors, or the public at large, your corporate brand is key to any campaign and must, by necessity, reflect your corporate character. Corporate character is defined to a large degree by a company's sense of social responsibility.

According to Walker Research, "seventy percent of consumers say they would not buy, no matter the discount, from a company they do not perceive to be 'socially responsible'. This significant majority of U.S. consumers is still very much concerned with price, quality, and service. But [consumers] are also concerned with how a company practices business, treats employees, invests in the community, cares for the environment, and maintains stability.

"Corporations, scrambling to react, implement strategies to address a variety of concerns—cause-related marketing campaigns, philanthropic efforts, new packaging to reflect 'green advertising', the employment of ethics officers, and social responsibility reports for shareholders."[6]

Walker Research tells us that "stakeholder decisions (see Exhibit 11–2) to purchase from, become employed by, or invest in a particular company [are] dependent upon the public's perception of [the company] as a good corporate citizen.

"So concerned are consumers with a corporation's character that more than three-fourths say they are currently avoiding or

WHAT IS CORPORATE SOCIAL RESPONSIBILITY?

Business factors rank as follows to reflect their importance relative to corporate social responsibility:

1. Business practices
2. Community support
3. Employee treatment
4. Quality
5. Environment
6. Service
7. Price
8. Convenience
9. Stability

The Top 20 Activities/Characteristics of Socially Responsible Companies

- Makes products that are safe
- Does not pollute air or water
- Obeys the law in all aspects of business
- Promotes honest/ethical employee behavior
- Commits to safe workplace policies
- Does not use misleading, deceptive advertising
- Upholds stated policy banning discrimination
- Utilizes "environmentally friendly" packaging
- Protects employees against sexual harassment
- Recycles within company
- Shows no past record of questionable activity
- Responds quickly to customer problems
- Maintains waste reduction program
- Provides/pays portion of medical
- Promotes energy conservation program
- Helps displaced workers with placement
- Gives money to charitable/educational causes
- Utilizes only biodegradable/recycling materials
- Employs friendly/courteous/responsive personnel
- Tries continually to improve quality

© 1994 WALKER: RESEARCH & ANALYSIS, L.P.®

refusing to buy from a business, 48 percent due to business practices. Workers say they look importantly on social responsibility in a potential employer. And 26 percent of potential investors say it's extremely important in making investment decisions. In fact, 21 percent of those who already invest always check on business practices, values and ethics before doing so."

Social responsibility and corporate citizenship are key building blocks for a strong corporate reputation. Reputation is part and parcel of corporate brand and prerequisite for those companies aspiring to attain or maintain leadership positions. This is especially true in those highly competitive industries where quality, price, and service are not differentiating factors.

The company then that wants to have a competitive advantage to be able to withstand a corporate crisis will pay strict attention to its social responsibilities. It will take particular pains to analyze periodically its reputation as well as those of its competitors. In doing so, the company will mark and measure the various elements that drive the perceptions of their reputation, and will put these findings to work for them in the marketplace.

By supporting publicly a socially responsible cause, with its obvious implications of positive corporate character, such a company takes a major step toward defining its essence and beliefs and establishing a powerful corporate brand.

NOTES

1. Don Phillips, "Bringing Truck Lobby to Screeching Halt," *The Washington Post,* June 15, 1991.
2. Charles W. Bailey, "How Washington Insiders Ambushed Mickey Mouse," *Washington Monthly,* December, 1994.
3. Rick Atkinson, "Germany, Church of Scientology Feuding in Print and Political Arena," *The Washington Post,* January 30, 1995.
4. Ibid.
5. Jonathon S. Baskin, Nissan North America, Inc., "Are the Days of Green Marketing Numbered?" ANA/*The Advertiser,* Summer 1992.
6. © 1994 Walker: Research Analysis, L. P.®

CHAPTER TWELVE

INTERACTIVE MEDIA . . . AND STRONG BRAND POSITION

"I believe branding takes on more importance than ever in an interactive environment. The Internet, for instance, affords a business the opportunity to create a brand synergy that has been very difficult to achieve through traditional media. Disparate products and services can be offered through one 'door', one point of access that bears the brand. People enter that door and, perhaps for the first time, experience the full breadth and depth of the brand."

    —RUPERT L. SMITH
        DIRECTOR—COMMUNICATIONS FOR ELECTRONIC TECHNOLOGIES
        GTE CORPORATION

Addressing the subject of leveraging the brand would be incomplete without discussing interactive media, the newest communication channels. The rules are different; the interactive mindset is different. It's a totally new environment that warrants careful consideration for inclusion in the chain of marketing and communications.

Because interactive media are so new, so explosive in their growth and potential, and are still evolving—some of the specifics here may be outdated by the time this book is published. Nevertheless, the principles expressed here will endure.

GTE's Rupert Smith (now president of Webpolish) sets the stage for this discussion. "Interactive media are two-way communication channels. They are often referred to as 'new media' because the traditional print and broadcast media have been historically one-way channels of communication.

"Interactive media are broadly defined. In addition to computer related forms, they can include infomercials and home shopping television networks, among others."

Computer-based interactive media include:

The Internet—A global network of interconnected computer networks that can be used to send or retrieve information. The information ranges from plain text to music to video. Most people access the "Net" through their organization's in-house computer network or directly through local service providers. The hottest part of the Internet currently is the World Wide Web, which is being transformed from a hyperlinked network of billboards into a true multimedia experience.

On-line services—Companies such as America Online, CompuServe, Prodigy, and Microsoft Network offer a variety of informational, educational, and entertainment services accessible by anyone with a computer, a modem, and the appropriate software. They also have begun to offer access to the Internet.

CD-ROM—It stands for compact disc—read only memory. These are like music CDs, but can hold much more information, including video and text in addition to music. CD-ROM drives play CD-ROM discs.

E-mail—Electronic mail. In its simplest form, e-mail is a text message carried by a computer network.

Video conferencing—With the rapid growth of home computers and telecommunicating, video conferencing from the desk-top should be one of the hottest of the interactive media within the next two years.

For all the press coverage and general hype about interactive media, they are still media, channels of communication to convey messages. As with the printed page or a television show, use of them should be determined by your objective, target audience, and message. Does the majority of your customers use computers? If they do not, then interactive media could well mean a considerable waste of your money.

THE IMPACT OF INTERACTIVE

Some sociologists and economists say that the advent of a digital, interactive communications environment will have greater impact on how we live and work than did the Industrial Revolution. Interactive media are the tools of this information age.

Consider these statistics:

- There are 108.96 million PC users, 54 percent of the U.S. population age 16 and over.

- Two out of five households now have a personal computer, according to a survey conducted by the Electronic Industries Association for the Consumer Electronics Manufacturers Association."

- Thirty-five million people have accessed the Internet, which is accessible in more than 100 countries.

- Depending on the source, males represent 51 to 68 percent of users, females 32 to 42 percent. Ethnicity: 71 percent white; 15 percent African-American; 10 percent Hispanic; 5 percent Asian.

- The number of registered commercial sites on the Internet increased more than 500 percent in 1996.[1]

- The number of CD-ROM drives in use rose by 140 percent in 1994 to nearly 27 million. More than 90 million CD-ROM discs were sold during the year, up 161 percent.

- There are 28 million e-mail "mailboxes" in the United States. The average number of daily messages per mailbox is about 20. This is expected to double within the next two years.

THE GREAT INFORMATION RESOURCE

Generally speaking, many of the companies making significant money through interactive media are those in computer or computer-related businesses. But this has not stopped thousands of other corporations from rushing into these exciting new media, particularly the Internet.

The Internet is the great information resource. Just about anything you want is accessible through the Net. And you not only have information retrieval, but you have transaction capability as well. With television commercials costing many thousands of dollars a minute, more and more companies are establishing their own home pages on the Internet through the World Wide Web. The advertiser can build as shallow or as deep an Internet presence as he or she chooses. You can provide videos of your products with accompanying graphics, sound, informational text, 800-numbers, addresses, etc.—and at a comparatively low cost.

THE WORLD WIDE WEB EXPERIENCE

Rupert Smith describes the World Wide Web as "the most user friendly part of the Internet." Its data is offered in 'point and click' form. Each page contains clickable links to other pages that may be located within the original site accessed or anywhere in the world.

According to Forrester Research, based in Cambridge, Massachusetts, on-line shopping will jump to $6.6 billion in 2000, up from $518 million in 1996. And business-to-business selling will rise to $117 billion from $1 billion in 1996, predicts International Data Corp., based in Framingham, Massachusetts.[2]

Most, if not all, of the nearly 3,000 businesses that have already established a site on the World Wide Web are still going through a learning process in this new interactive media domain. However, their experience thus far offers lessons that can be very valuable to other companies now just opening up a Web site.

WEB 101

Other Web locations or information that you choose to link to should be relevant to the content of your Web site and imaginatively conceived. For example, a shoe sales site might have a link to a shoe polish outlet and also, perhaps, to research on the human foot.

A Web site is not something you build and then sit back to admire. It is a major corporate commitment. The technical support and user response requirements are not only ongoing but will increase if your site is successful.

A Web site should not be launched until it has been tested by representative focus groups. Internet travelers have high expectations and are impatient. If your site does not make a favorable impression on their first visit, it is unlikely they will return. The best Web sites offer not only a feedback mechanism for visitors, but also forums in which visitors can exchange thoughts.

COMPANY-WIDE INFORMATION ON DEMAND

External audiences are not a company's only Internet targets. Employees as well may be reached by sites on the Web. Reports *Business Week:* "Businesses of every kind have found that the Internet's World Wide Web is a great way to get information to customers or investors. Now, they're finding that using the same technology internally—on intranets—can dramatically improve, [employee] communications, unlock hidden information, and transform organizations. The Web, it turns out, is an inexpensive yet powerful alternative to other forms of internal communications, including conventional computer setups.

"Federal Express Corp.'s customer Web site has become a legendary success story, letting 12,000 customers per day click their way through Web pages to pinpoint their parcels—instead of asking a human operator to do it for them and saving up to $2 million a year by some estimates.

"'We saw the success of the package tracking site and [wondered] what we could do on the inside', says Susan Goeldner, manager of Internet Technology for Federal Express. The answer: a lot. Today there are 60 Web sites running inside the company, most created for and by employees."[3]

FedEx is not alone in its use of intranets. Many corporations, after getting their feet wet with public Web sites that promote company products and services, are seizing the Web as a swift way to streamline and even transform their organizations.

One natural advantage of an intranet is its ability to reduce substantially the use of paper. And Web browsers run on any type of computer, so the same information is available for viewing by any employee. Procedure manuals, training materials, directories, and all sorts of company documents can be converted to electronic form on the Web and updated both frequently and inexpensively.

But that's not all intranets can accomplish. By presenting information in the same way to every computer, they can combine all the company computers, software, and databases into a single system that enables employees to access pertinent information wherever it is located.

By thus breaking down "walls" within the corporation, intranets contribute immeasurably to the full integration of internal corporate communications, a key step in assuring the understanding and success of a corporate branding program with all employees.

IS INTERACTIVE FOR YOU?

The starting point in all marketing communication these days has to do with societal trends. You examine the legitimate trends and then look for the marriage of those trends with existing technology and sometimes with government regulations. Wherever these coincide you find the greatest marketing opportunities.

As you might imagine, there is a lot of eagerness right now by many companies to become interactive, to get onto the Internet and into CD-ROMs, to do electronic mail and video conferencing—to participate in all the different forms that interactive takes. But interactive may not be right for everyone.

Warns Christine MacKenzie, manager of corporate advertising at Chrysler Corporation, "Those who think they know the technology are walking before they can crawl."[4] In other words, too many companies are taking the big jump into interactive without fully understanding all of its implications and ramifications.

Writing in *Advertising Age,* Scott Donaton offers, "Message to marketers who have established—or are in the process of setting up—sites on the Internet: Why are you doing this?

"This is the one question every company should ask itself two or three thousand times before giving the green light to an internal task force or ad agency or anyone else to set them up with a home page on the World Wide Web. If the answer is 'Because everyone else is', keep your money in the bank.

"It's not to say marketers shouldn't be experimenting with new media outlets. Of course they should. And marketers will clearly play a key role in shaping Internet culture as the global network of networks emerges as a mainstream medium.

"But marketers should not be exploiting technology because it's there. They should be figuring out whether and how the Internet can help them meet marketing goals."[5]

DON'T IGNORE BASIC MARKETING PRINCIPLES

With this very much in mind, Rupert Smith has developed a model that can help a company address its marketing and communications needs, determine whether or not they should indeed go interactive, and, if so, which of the new media to use.

He notes: "People forget that basic marketing and communications principles still apply. You might actually harm your company by going interactive. You still need to go through the chain of establishing your brand position and goals, identifying the targets of those goals, setting communications objectives, and choosing media and other vehicles that can get the job done.

"If you follow this model, you'll make effective communications choices. Maybe they will involve interactive media. Maybe not. The point is, however, that people are moving so fast that in many instances they ignore basic marketing and communications processes that must still be followed. They make the jump all the way to some form of communication, be it on CD-ROM or an ad on Internet, without going through the steps that will ensure their choice is the most effective way for them to go.

"Good marketers and communicators will look past the sexiness of interactive media and evaluate them as business tools. If it is then determined that interactive makes sense in terms of a company's brand position, goals, and target audiences, the opportunities offered by this new form of media are incredible."

WHERE IS IT ALL GOING?

Technological changes are occurring so rapidly that the only safe prediction of where we are going is just about anywhere the innovative minds of marketers can take us.

Consider financial services. The financial community now recognizes that the future of their particular products and services lies with an on-line environment. Banking is already moving into the home. Chase Manhattan, for instance, offers their Chase Direct service via the personal computer and telephone. By e-mail, one can download current information on both checking and savings as well as order checks to be sent to pay any and all bills. Loan applications can be taken by telephone.

This is only a beginning. Studies show that banks are increasing their spending on technology, while their branches' share of transactions decreases. Home banking, representing only 1 percent of transactions in 1994, will account for an estimated 6 percent by 1997.[6] These are small figures today, but highly indicative of what is to come.

Such changes in banking technology and procedure are bound to have a dynamic effect on the corporate brand of any bank that offers home banking service, bearing directly on the vital corporate declarations of "Who we are" and "What we believe." But dramatic changes in corporate branding will not be limited to the banking industry.

COMPUTER-BASED SHOPPING

Catalogers, too, are going on-line. Writes *Advertising Age*'s Gary Levin: "2Market, a company formed by America Online, Apple Computer, and Medior, [has introduced] a new version of the catalog disc, also called 2Market. 'We're aiming at home consumers who aren't necessarily technocentric,' said Michael Minigan, vice president for business development.

"Merchant mix includes 27 catalogs and 2,500 products, including recorded music selections promoted with music-video clips. 2Market will test a variety of pricing strategies, including sending the discs for free.

"The CD-ROM version of the catalog opens with a digitized female guide, who [describes] in a 5-minute opening spiel the hassle of retail shopping, then walks users through a menu screen that allows them to choose among several shopping methods.

"A single vendor's entire product line can be displayed sequentially in pages; a particular item can be retrieved from any of several catalogs; and a personal shopper displays gifts selected by price range, subject interests, gift occasions and age groups. Individual items can be marked and quickly retrieved for later perusal. Catalogers view this and other interactive products as a way to tap new customers who shy away from traditional print catalogs."[7]

From AAAA's *BackChannel*, "The third edition of America Online's CD-ROM shopping disk, issued for the 1995 holiday season, contained the on-line catalogs of 19 marketers such as Starbucks Coffee, FAO Schwarz, and Eddie Bauer. The jazziest offerings, though, belong to the multimedia vendors—Tower Records, Voyager Co., and Windham Hill records. Users enticed by the picture of Windham Hill recording artists Tuck & Patti, for example, could listen to audio samples from their albums, or play a 30-second QuickTime video."[8]

ELECTRONIC PUBLISHING ON THE INTERNET

In a completely different approach, a major publisher of high-tech magazines has undertaken a particularly ambitious Internet effort. CMP Publications has introduced an ad-supported service called TechWeb, an Internet site that features content from each of the publisher's 16 titles and ancillary business units. This is an aggressive corporate commitment to embrace electronic publishing.

"Internet users can gain entry to any of the magazines' individual areas. . . . Users will be able to call up news and current issues, download multimedia files, send e-mail to writers and editors, and access up to six months of back issues using advanced searching tools.

"While each home page [has] its own look and feel, they [are] all connected by hypertext links, enabling users to jump between publications at the click of a mouse. Other bells and whistles include information on CMP conferences and the ability to subscribe to publications or change a subscription address."[9]

CMP is not the only publisher involved with interactive. Among others, Time, Inc. has launched Pathfinder, featuring several of their publications, including *Time, Money,* and *Vibe.* McGraw Hill has created a new Information Services Group and is exploring Internet opportunities for *Business Week* and other of their properties. More than 1,000 newspapers are on-line, and the venerable *New York Times* offers an ad-supported Internet version of its daily Times Fax, complementing its @Times on America Online.

A CONCEPT FOR JUST ABOUT EVERYONE

As broad a concept as interactive may be, the number and variety of companies now involved seem even broader. Miller Brewing, Reuben H. Donnelley, Nynex, Dow Chemical, NBC, Club Med, Saturn, British Airways, Sony, American Express, Chrysler, Best Western, and Campbell Soup are but a baker's dozen from an impressive and ever-lengthening list.

Flowers and greeting cards are sold through interactive. Trekkies have visited an Internet site that touted the Paramount Pictures release, *Star Trek—Generations.* Online golfers play against each other on computer replicas of real courses. These cyberspace golfers are creating a whole new market for software companies, corporate sponsors, and advertisers.

Even the Super Bowl has gone on-line. In what the ABC-TV network called the first interactive Super Bowl—XXIX—America Online subscribers were able, according to *Advertising Age,* "to download photos and video clips taken from an on-field camera. Subscribers [were also] able to play along with the big game by using NTN Communications' QB1." [10]

E-MAIL FOR FREE

Juno Online Services L.P. now offers free electronic mail service, the ability to send and receive messages without paying the usual membership and usage fees that on-line services normally charge for e-mail. In exchange, Juno customers agree to supply information about their lifestyles, reading habits, plans to purchase big ticket items, and other demographics. According to Stuart Elliott in the *New York Times,* "They also agree to receive advertisements, which come in color, change about every 30 seconds, and typically occupy only a portion of the computer screen.

"'Millions of people use the Internet for nothing but e-mail,' said Charles Ardai, president of Juno. 'I'm confident we can get to many of them. The question is how many and how quickly.'

"The primary way to accomplish that, he added, 'is to build a brand identity.' So in a consumer and trade campaign which involves print advertisements and direct mail, Juno asserts 'E-mail was meant to be free.'"[11]

A number of national marketers have already signed with Juno. These include Welch Foods, SmithKline Beecham, Quaker Oats, Columbia House, owned by Sony and Time Warner, Lands' End, and the Miramax Films unit of the Walt Disney Company. An exciting new branding opportunity, ads offer users elaborate graphics and extended sales pitches, accessible by clicking on an icon.

ANYTHING ELSE YOU NEED TO KNOW?

Is there anything else you should know about interactive media? Definitely yes! A whole lot. As Rupert Smith comments, "Most of it has to do with 'constructing' interactive media and learning the rules of using it, particularly the Internet. But if your objective, target, and message together make a case for interactive media, then you should obtain this additional knowledge. Talk to the firms and individuals who specialize in it. And if you haven't already, subscribe to an on-line service. See for yourself what all the excitement is about.

"Interactive media are exciting new communications channels that offer real-time as well as responsive two-way communications with customers, employees, and other constituencies. They are potentially powerful vehicles for a corporate branding program.

"But interactive media should always be considered along with the conventional media—print, radio, television, direct mail, and interpersonal. Communications plans of the most successful businesses do not exclude one medium because it is traditional nor include another simply because it is new and exciting."

In the next 10 to 15 years, advertisers will be forced to use a more segmented approach and tailor their messages to highly fragmented consumer audiences. Says Robert H. Ducoffe, assistant professor of marketing at Baruch College, "The emergence of customized communications as an effective and more efficient form of advertising will eventually dominate mass communications.

"Electronic media is proliferating rapidly. Consumers will have more options to choose from, forcing advertisers toward more narrow approaches."[12]

It seems a sure bet that the new interactive media in all their forms are going to play an increasingly prominent role in advertising's future. Your company—and your corporate brand—is bound to be touched by electronic media in one way or another.

NOTES

1. Gary Visgadis, "On-line's Elusive Face," *USA Today,* October 9, 1996. Sources: IntelliQuest, Yankelovich, Georgia Institute of Technology. See also Steve Lohr, "The Great Unplugged Masses Confront the Future," *New York Times,* April 21, 1996.
2. David Stipp, "The Birth of Digital Commerce," *Fortune,* December 9, 1996.
3. Amy Cortese, "Here Comes The Intranet," *Business Week,* February 26, 1996.
4. Christine MacKenzie, *Advertising Age,* February 20, 1995.
5. Scott Donaton, "Mucking Up Marketing on the 'Net'," *Advertising Age,* January 23, 1995.
6. B. G. Yovovich, "Banking on Home Interactivity," *Advertising Age,* January 16, 1995.
7. Gary Levin, "Catalogers Take Wares 2Market," *Advertising Age,* November 21, 1994.
8. "Interactivity," *BackChannel,* the Interactivity Newsletter of the American Association of Advertising Agencies, February 1996, Vol. 2 No. 1.
9. Scott Donaton, "CMP Spins TechWeb on the 'Net'," *Advertising Age,* November 14, 1994.
10. Debra Aho Williamson, "Kicking Off the First Interactive Super Bowl," *Advertising Age,* January 23, 1995.
11. Stuart Elliott, "Advertising / Juno would be delighted to handle your E-mail free. . . . ", *New York Times,* April 22,1996.
12. "Study Reveals Advertising's Future," *Integrated Marketing,* April 6, 1995.

CORPORATE BRANDING AND THE CEO

CHAPTER THIRTEEN

CORPORATE GROWTH VERSUS STATUS QUO

"There is nothing more difficult to carry out, nor more doubtful of success than to initiate a new order of things. For the reformer has enemies in all those who profit by the old order."

—NICCOLO MACHIAVELLI

Michael Allen, an astute analyst of how companies grow, writes: "The challenge of leading a growth enterprise requires a higher level of managerial leadership talent than that of maintaining the status quo. The reason is that rapid growth dramatically expands the complexity of the CEO's job."[1]

Unfortunately, too many corporate managements are basically content with the status quo. They simply do not appreciate the potential value of a corporate brand. Perhaps they are misled by the illusion of growth caused by the high inflation of the '70s and '80s. Their businesses are profitable, and growth investments, including that of a corporate brand, are seen only as an imprudent risk.

Other possible explanations for this apparent reluctance to grow their companies fell into three categories:

- Internal politics—i.e., brand managers, divisional executives, and others with their own agendas, their own budgets, their own little empires to build, are loathe to lose any of it. Why should they want to integrate their programs with someone else's? They might lose control!

- External influences—most notably advertising and public relations agencies. Whenever more than one is employed by the same company, rivalries and jealousies may ensue. Each agency looks to grab for itself a bigger piece of the pie, and each has its own idea as to what the corporate message should be and how best to present it.

- What I term "inexplicable" reasons—a thousand-and-one of them as to why a corporate brand is not promoted and why company marketing and communications strategies are not coordinated. The reasons may be economic: "We simply can't afford it"; of historical persuasion: "We tried it twenty years ago and it didn't work"; traditional: "If it ain't broke don't fix it"; and the perennial standbys: "We just don't need it" and "It will never happen here."

But there is one additional reason, perhaps most devastating of all. It is the lack of corporate will to grow. Some corporate cultures are mired in a malaise that stymies strategic insight and imagination. Their CEOs are too paralyzed or unwilling to define the vision and inspire their associates.

A DROUGHT OF INSIGHT AND INNOVATION

Even when they have vision, however, many CEOs simply don't know how to communicate it clearly and vigorously to the organization. No wonder a survey of the corporate landscape over the past few years reveals large barren areas with little growth. Corporation after corporation has suffered from a drought of strategic insight and creative innovation.

Says a noted business consultant, Michael Allen of the Michael Allen Company: "The cancer of eroding growth starts eating away at a business well before the symptoms are evident in weak sales or earnings."[2]

He adds: "Company culture, as reflected by employee behavior, does not prize growth. This is most true when a 'mature' business dominates a company and the successful managers are those who nurtured its senior years. Profitability is revered. Growth expenditures are a risk. These managers, perhaps, forget that a business is most profitable just before it starts to decline."[3]

The antidote is to restore growth, Allen says, by "expanding the value delivered to customers. Benchmark studies of 'star' growth businesses show that their success is rooted in an innovative value proposition, and that they sustain rapid growth by constantly pushing forward the 'value' frontier. Growth businesses must therefore invest in proprietary understanding of changing customer perceptions of value and must ensure that they have the muscle to create new value in response."

I believe that the quest for value can best be achieved by establishing a dynamic corporate brand, which attests to a commitment to new value and invites new customer perceptions and reactions. Unfortunately, too many companies have not yet discovered the principle of corporate branding and seem content, instead, to settle for the status quo.

THE WILL OF THE LEADERSHIP

Corporate branding is just not possible without an inherent corporate will to grow. Any lack of such will starts by nature at the top. The active, positive leadership of the chief executive officer is imperative, and a major aspect of that leadership is the ability to communicate with clarity and authority.

The CEO without an instinctive, driving will for corporate growth will not be able to handle the complexities of growth management. A personal lack of imagination, philosophical ties to past successes, and complacency with the status quo become deadly obstacles in the CEO's own path and in the path of any plans for corporate branding.

And without the vision and enthusiasm of the CEO, the management team will not hear, comprehend, or care about the corporate message. Corporate branding will be, in their eyes, only a challenge to personal agendas.

The successful chief executive officer must balance the imperative of immediate profits with the need to invest wisely and aggressively for the future. He or she must champion a continuing improvement of existing operations and at the same time restructure the way in which the company does business. He must inspire the company team, build its self-confidence, and yet have the foresight and courage to make changes in the team when necessary.

One CEO who successfully led his company through a remarkable turnaround was C. Ray Holman of Mallinckrodt Medical. Having restructured the business around their markets in 1988, Holman took the next step in 1992 "by globally consolidating these business units—helping us to become truly global in our thinking, our actions, and our sensitivity to markets in every part of the world. The magnitude of change is large, indeed. Huge amounts of management time and energy are required."[4]

By Holman's remarkable actions Mallinckrodt Medical was transformed, and Holman was promoted to president and chief executive officer of the Imcera Group, Mallinckrodt's parent company (which he has since changed to Mallinckrodt).

THE WILL OF THE ORGANIZATION

Not all business leaders, however, have either the spirit or the inclination to follow such an agenda. Perhaps they deceive themselves about the current need for growth for survival, preferring to harken back to an era when profits came more easily, more automatically. Perhaps new demands on corporate leadership seem just too great. Perhaps their company culture simply does not accept the potential of a corporate brand.

R. Donald Gamache, business consultant, points out, "Most companies are organized functionally, and each unit is headed by an individual with clear goals and responsibilities—and sometimes hidden agendas. Therefore, in most companies, expecting a single function to make something new happen that will inevitably impinge on other functions is not realistic.

"And companies almost always have a 'cultural' bias, that is, they are primarily led and oriented in the direction of technology, manufacturing, sales, and so forth. Yet any new opportunity will require the participation and support of many or most functions to be successful.

"The organization with a strong will to grow must recognize clearly the need for a concerted effort to identify and implement new growth opportunities. Many organizations give only lip service to the need for growth, so tangible results never occur."[5]

Comments Helena Rubenstein, managing director of the London-based Brand Consultancy: "Our idea is to look at brands and branding as a core business process, not just a communications process, and encourage a much more accountable approach. We are concerned that marketing departments and finance departments don't speak the same language, and that decisions affecting the marketing budget might be made by people who don't understand why or how brands work."[6]

THE WILL OF THE MARKETPLACE

The fault, however, may not necessarily lie completely with old-style and probably unimaginative executives. The economics of the last decade or so have left a great deal to be desired, and may indeed have transmitted misleading signals to many business leaders.

Says Michael Allen: "Regrettably, many businesses have found their growth stunted by the financially driven strategies of the '80s and by the restructured marketplace of the '90s.

"They become preoccupied with survival and with the preservation of financial viability. Often this triggers excessive attention to infrastructure reduction, i.e., futures are cut back; jobs downscaled; juniors given assignments over their heads; management stress (is focused) on the quick, cheap fix.

"The consequence has been an accelerating downward spiral of dwindling real growth, market-share erosion, margins squeezed by price pressure, slowing productivity gains, short-fall from profit targets, and declining share value."[7]

WARNING SIGNS

Apart from the hard facts of the bottom line, how can you spot a company in trouble? Here's a short list of distress signals:

- CEO offers little or no vision for company
- No communicator on senior management team
- Senior management concentrates on production or financial issues
- Lethargic, disinterested employees
- Major differences among management
- Most customer contact is with lower levels of employees
- Inconsistent media stories about company
- Stagnant stock price or low trading volume

There are other signs but these are especially symptomatic of corporate ill health. Note in particular: "No CEO vision" and "No management communicator." Such signals portend a sick, if not dying, corporate brand.

CORPORATE ANOREXIA

Reviewing *Competing for the Future* in *Business Week,* John A. Byrne writes: "Downsizing, the authors say, is the equivalent of 'corporate anorexia.' It can make a company thinner, but not necessarily healthier.

"[The authors] argue, for example, that the most aggressive downsizers in recent years are largely a 'rogues gallery of under-managed or wrongly managed companies.' Indeed, the inability of many managers to look ahead for ways to reinvent their industries has led to both costly blunders and monumental catch-up costs."[8]

For whatever reasons, including the vagaries of the recent economy, some companies simply find it difficult to grow. Not fully understanding the concept of real growth, some may even believe they *are* growing.

R. Donald Gamache suggests that restructuring can cloud the issue of real growth: "I'm really convinced that as time passes, shareholders will put much more emphasis on real growth in balance with earnings per share growth.

"Many companies have lived off improvements in productivity in recent years. Leaner organizational structures have been achieved through various restructuring efforts that have squeezed improved productivity from existing resources. Consequently, earnings per share [may have developed] nicely, but not from real growth, not enough from the truly new."[9]

Michael Allen describes real growth this way: "Growth oriented companies demonstrate strong beliefs in a market-driven philosophy. This means growth starts with the belief that customers have a limitless need for greater value. Robust growth validates the value provided to customers, expands jobs and allows productivity improvements that boost profitability. It is, therefore, the primary source of shareowner and social wealth. Without growth, a company will eventually fail itself and its constituents."[10]

PUSHING FORWARD THE VALUE FRONTIER

Business failure doesn't just happen all of a sudden, of course. At times when business budgets are strung taut and financial performance goals leave little room for risk investment, corporate growth becomes the first victim.

Early detection of the symptoms and intelligent treatment are crucial. Studies of robust growth businesses show they sustain rapid growth by constantly pushing forward the "value" frontier, i.e., expanding the value delivered to customers. Central to customer perception of this new value is corporate branding with its unified, positive message.

Some part of the newly created value must go to customers to "buy" market share from competitors, and some part must go to the innovator as a reward for creating value. This is why although so-called "me too" products may be relatively easy to market, even be less expensive, they are also rarely successful. There is simply no new brand value to be shared by consumers and producers.

BEATING SWORDS INTO PLOWSHARES

One of the major consequences of the end of the Cold War has been its impact on defense industry-based companies. The resulting shrinkage of defense spending has compelled many companies, large and small, to recast their corporate branding. Former DOD suppliers are scrambling to repackage themselves, seeking new peacetime marketing directions.

Years of supplying parts and weapons to government, with little emphasis on cost control, insulated many of these companies from the harsh economics of private industry. Corporations that have been accustomed to a single customer must get used to a whole new kind of marketing. They must redefine the answers to "who we are" and "what we believe."

They are searching for new target audiences and learning to communicate new messages to them. With a clear vision of their future, such companies must project new reputations to new markets . . . reputations with such favorable characteristics as quality, value, dependability, and even community mindedness.

In other words, they must actively seek new and more realistic corporate branding. It's a matter of survival.

Whatever the economy, no matter how difficult the marketing environment, there are countless ways to take a company into the future, and even change that future. Countless ways to help a company succeed and grow. All of which adds up to countless ways to help a company revitalize an existing corporate brand or create a totally new one.

Even small companies can create and use a corporate brand to succeed and grow, just as large ones. We'll examine several of these in the next chapter.

But there can be no continuing and successful corporate will to grow—for either a large or small company—without the CEO's recognition of the need for corporate branding, complete understanding of its function, and ability to communicate and sell that concept to his or her organization.

NOTES

1. Michael Allen, "The Resurgence of Business Growth as an Objective," The Michael Allen Company, 1992.
2. Ibid.
3. Michael Allen, "Revitalizing Corporate Growth," The Michael Allen Company.
4. Allen, "Resurgence of Business Growth."
5. R. Donald Gamache and Robert Lawrence Kuhn, *The Creativity Infusion* (New York: Harper Business Division, Harper-Collins, 1989).
6. Stuart Elliott, "Advertising," *New York Times,* May 23, 1994.
7. Allen, "Resurgence of Business Growth."
8. John A. Byrne, "'Corporate Anorexia': A Lack-Of-Foresight Saga," *Business Week,* September 19, 1994, review of Gary Hamel and C. K. Prahalad, *Competing for the Future* (Harvard Business School Press, 1994).
9. Gamache, *The Creativity Infusion.*
10. Allen, "Resurgence of Business Growth."

CHAPTER FOURTEEN

THE ROLE OF THE CEO

"An army of lions led by a sheep is no match for an army of sheep led by a lion."

—WINSTON CHURCHILL

"The fast track to the executive suite is now faster—not to mention more unpredictable and a lot riskier," says Amanda Bennett of *The Wall Street Journal*. Bennett continues , "At company after company, as old-style chiefs are tossed out and replaced by surprise successors, middle managers are finding that many of the old truisms about climbing the ladder to the top are no longer true. Knowing your own job isn't enough; you need broad experience. One high-placed mentor won't help much; a fast mover will need several. Sticking around headquarters to be seen doesn't cut it any more either. Foreign experience, although still frequently seen by up-and-coming employees as a career kiss of death, is rapidly becoming essential.

"And forget about the straight climb to the top of the company you started with. Increasingly, the fast track up will be a zigzag through different companies."[1]

WHICH LADDER IS UP?

Wide career experience becomes more and more desirable in companies that require a continuous parade of executives with varying experiences and viewpoints.

No longer does the course to the executive suite rise straight up a single ladder labeled Engineering, Manufacturing, Finance, Marketing, or such. More often these days it takes a number of zigs and zags through a variety of disciplines, product lines, corporate experiences, and even foreign countries.

THE BROADEST POSSIBLE RANGE OF SKILLS

More and more companies want to have senior executives who are equipped with the broadest possible range of skills, according to Robert Lear, former CEO of the F&M Schaefer Corporation and currently Executive-in-Residence at Columbia Business School. In his recent book, *How to Turn Your MBA into a CEO*, Lear describes how the demands of overseeing a large corporation are such that CEOs increasingly need to be able to deal competently with everything from finance, marketing and operations to control, planning, research, and public relations—in other words, all of the business trades. "Executives who have become too specialized in one segment either do not get chosen for a top slot or have an extremely difficult indoctrination and adjustment period," he writes.

The resistance to overspecialization, furthermore, can be seen in the fact that most companies currently pursue conscious programs of job rotation, according to Lear, who adds: "Most of our multinational corporations want their top executives to have worked directly with foreign problems at some time during their career."[2]

"At AT&T in the past," says Harold Burlingame, senior vice president of human resources, "we had people who were viewed against a static set of assumptions: good leadership, good people skills, good understanding of financials.

"But now that list will say: the capacity to build joint ventures offshore, to take new and struggling businesses and make them successful, to take a work group and totally redefine the mission, to handle a strategic attack from a competitor and come up with alternatives."[3]

COMMUNICATION IS A MUST

Today's new CEO needs to be multitalented and multidimensional. As one responsible for an entire corporation, the more background and training the CEO has, the better equipped he or she will be to meet the challenges of the future. That old fashioned ladder just doesn't reach the top as easily or as often as it used to.

Broad experience, foreign experience, diversified company experience: All are important for today's chief executive officer. But—and this is key—none of it makes much difference in the long run if he can't communicate it to others.

Without communication from the top down, players on the management team will not be able to see the vision and catch the flame, much less understand and exploit it. Nor will the CEO be able to carry out a plan for corporate branding and growth fully, if at all, no matter how well conceived.

The CEO must know how to communicate, because, for all of his or her position and power, a CEO cannot function in a vacuum. He must know how to communicate experience and knowledge, feelings and vision, in such a manner as to move and energize the employees. He must have the genuine, visceral support of the company's top executives—the movers, the shakers, the decision makers—not to mention the rank and file.

It goes without saying that no corporate branding program can succeed without the clear, articulated support of the chief executive officer. An informal study I have completed identifies the background and experience of CEOs with good corporate branding skills. Interestingly enough, they can come from just about any business arena. They simply understand the value of communication.

THREE MANDATES

At a recent roundtable conference of CEOs, Russell L. Carson, a general partner of the investment management firm of Welsh, Carson, Anderson & Stowe, made the following remarks: "We give three principal mandates to the people who run our companies.

"First, the CEO must set a vision for the company that describes the business; its customers; its products; its future growth; and its investment, research and development, and acquisitions strategies.

"Next, the CEO must manage the business. The larger the company, the more that management has to be done by delegation. Nevertheless, at the end of the day, if the business is not being managed effectively, the CEO is the guy with his head on the block.

"Finally, the CEO has to be the company's principal communicator. He has to talk with employees, customers, external constituencies, and shareholders. He can't tell analysts and investors a story that falls apart afterward. But if he can tell the story well, and if he can produce what he says he's going to produce, the company's share price will reflect that."

Adds H. Brian Thompson of LCI International, at the same roundtable: "I believe CEOs can spend a good deal of time managing expectations and also create a vision for the company. Then he or she has to sell that story— not only in the marketplace but in the organization itself. If the employees don't believe it, the company won't perform."[4]

"THIS IS WHAT WE STAND FOR"

Many CEOs are willing to give time and attention to individual financial analysts, but find it a nuisance to give the attention required to create a corporate communications platform. When this is the case, the CEO should understand that when running a corporate campaign he can be speaking to all of the financial analysts who follow the industry, and to all other target audiences as well. What could show a greater commitment than to run a campaign that says: "This is the company. This is what we stand for. This is where we are going. This is how long it will take to get there!"

Any company seeking a new chief executive officer should bear in mind that if quality is to be the new paradigm, the time has come for a new kind of leadership: a leadership employing an entirely new set of skills in order for the company to progress successfully and profitably into the 21st century.

Writes Andrew Campbell, "The spirit of true leadership is the spirit that is not sure it is always right. Leaders who are not too sure they are right are leaders who listen.

"Leadership is about performance over time, not charisma—about responsibility, not privilege. It is about personal integrity and a strong belief in team play. It is about a willingness to take risks and not fear failure.

"It is a belief that true quality should define all relationships and that success results only when quality is present. Clearly, leaders must be multi-talented."[5]

THE PR EXECUTIVE AS CEO

It used to be that the road to the heights was trod almost exclusively by line executives. Staff executives were not often encouraged to pursue such dreams.

"That has changed," says Leonard Saffir in *Advertising Age*. "Lawyers, research scientists, human resource people—practitioners of these and other staff specialties can and do become CEOs of large organizations, although the bulk of these top jobs are still filled by persons from the conventional line backgrounds."[6]

Saffir sees even public relations executives moving into the top leadership positions in tomorrow's corporations. And why not? One of the attributes of a good PR person is the capacity to understand every phase of the operation, and be able to communicate his or her knowledge effectively.

In addition, the reaction of the public at large—and especially of all the target audiences—is of paramount consideration in most corporate planning. Indeed, it can be argued that someone who is gifted in analyzing and influencing public opinion is a particularly good choice to run a corporation. He or she will certainly understand the value of corporate branding, be in sympathy with its purposes, and able to communicate the concept effectively.

Will executives with public relations backgrounds be serving as CEOs in the 21st century? There is actually no fundamental reason why a PR person should not head up an IBM, General Electric, or General Motors.

CHANGE HAS NO CONSTITUENCY

Speculating on the characteristics of his own future successor as CEO of General Electric, Jack Welch had this to say: "Obviously, anybody who gets this job must have a vision for the company and must be capable of rallying people behind it.

"He or she has got to be very comfortable in a global environment, dealing with world leaders. Be comfortable dealing with people at all levels of the company. . . . Believe in the gut that people are the key to everything, and that change is not something you fear—it's something you relish.

"Anyone who is too inwardly focused, who doesn't cherish customers, who isn't open to change, isn't going to make it. One thing I've learned is that change has no constituency. People like the status quo. They like the way it *was*. When you start changing things, the good old days look better and better. You've got to be prepared for massive resistance.

"Finally, whoever gets [this] job will have to have what I call an 'edge'—an insatiable passion for winning and growing."[7]

It has been said that it takes a very special kind of leader to rise to the top of General Electric. Anyone who makes the grade, or comes anywhere near it, has faced a host of challenging circumstances and has worked inside more than one industry. No wonder GE's attitude toward leadership and its promotion criteria are so widely admired and closely monitored.

Perhaps that is why so many investors feel they have hit the jackpot when one of their companies announces the appointment of a CEO drawn from GE management. Nor is this an isolated situation; a surprising number of GE executives actually end up running major businesses.

But just *finding* the right leader isn't enough. Noted industrialist Alfred P. Sloan, Jr. said, "The maintenance of an unusually high standard of leadership in any industry is sometimes more difficult than the attainment of that leadership in the first place."

THE 24-HOUR QUARTERBACK

One of American business's most persistent cliches is that the CEO is like a professional football quarterback. After all, don't they usually call the shots, with success or failure riding on their shoulders? Perhaps, but it's an analogy that may have seen its time. Nowadays, the job of the chief executive officer is just too big, too complex.

The pro quarterback is concerned primarily with the offensive strategy of his team. When the team is on defense, he is off the field. But the CEO is in action *all* the time—24 hours a day, 365 days a year. He is totally responsible for the corporation, being as much concerned with "defensive" strategies as with the company's "offense." He is actually more coach than quarterback.

There are those who believe that the job of CEO has become far too big for one person. Growing shareholder and competitive pressures are making successful leadership more difficult than it has ever been. The result in a number of major corporations has been a splitting up of the jobs of chairman and CEO. Among other advantages, bifurcated leadership enables companies to change at the top while maintaining investor confidence.

Even in those corporations that have thus split the CEO's function, or who have created deputies with equal responsibility and power, the office of chief executive officer becomes increasingly demanding. The burden on a CEO makes it essential that he or she has established a deep familiarity with and experience in those many key areas that demand the time and talent of today's corporate leader.

Global perspective, customer focus, product intuitiveness, environmental awareness, resistance to bureaucracy, a will to grow and prosper corporately, and the ability to motivate others are some of the musts. Arguably, with such a full agenda the CEO who is unable to articulate his or her vision may accomplish little of worth and soon be out of a job. Perhaps more important, the company may lose step with competitors and even fail in the marketplace.

Without effective communication, vision is meaningless, corporate branding is impossible. And without corporate branding, it is a rare company that will succeed in the decades to come.

STRENGTHENING A COMPANY'S MENTAL MUSCLE

In a recent interview, Bruce Berger, Whirlpool's vice president for corporate affairs, commented, "There are things that happen in Clyde, Ohio, for example, that if our other manufacturing plants knew about them, no matter what they produced, they might be able to do something better—might be able to improve their own productivity. Or a new process in Italy or Brazil might improve quality at the Clyde or Evansville manufacturing operations.

"How do we keep such information moving across the organization? That's the most difficult kind of organizational communication there is—communicating horizontally.

"So, we're making an investment to better train our communications professionals in order to raise our standards and to link communications to business objectives. We also are providing management increasingly with training and the appropriate tools, techniques and approaches to drive communications across the organization.

"[We've launched] a new management publication whose purposes are to drive debate and thinking and to strengthen our mental muscle company-wide. We've implemented some electronic news systems to drive the speed and currency of communication. We have a seven step process model that we use globally to plan, implement, and measure communications strategies and projects; the process links communication to real business objectives.

"We're also piloting several technologies and have begun to expand our management communications training program and to move day-to-day communications accountabilities to individual managers, where it most properly belongs," Berger said.

"All of these efforts help, but we still have miles to go in communications and other areas to create the kind of working environment that produces the thinking, creativity, risk taking, productivity, and results that will set us apart regularly from the competition."

THE CONTINUING SPARK

When asked the importance of their CEO's ongoing support, Berger replied: "It [is] absolutely central. He was the spark that started it and is the continuing spark to keep it going. Without Dave Whitwam saying, 'This is important. . . . We're going to do it', it simply wouldn't happen. It's that vital."

Even in this age of communication, some CEOs don't have a clue. They simply don't understand that the ability to communicate effectively is the single most essential ingredient for success in today's corporate world. On the other hand, there are people like Whirlpool's Whitwam who not only understand but know how to put it all together.

Continues Berger, "When I interviewed with Dave Whitwam, he [told me] that he wanted to achieve two communication objectives for Whirlpool. The first was a global strategy for public relations so that the corporation would have a worldwide identification that would mean what we wanted it to mean. And we were starting from a zero recognition base outside North America.

"The other goal was for an employee communications strategy. He wanted all of our people to understand where we are going [so that we could] commit ourselves to making a full effort for the company. This would involve a massive change—a complete change of mindset, thinking, and understanding for all of our employees because none of us had been part of a global organization before.

"Whitwam's a man of significant vision. At the time he did not go into any lengthy explanation as to 'why', but he did say that the company might possibly be successful without a new external and internal identity or image, but it wouldn't be the kind of company he wanted."

DIRECTION STARTS AT THE TOP

External and internal images: the two halves of the complete corporate experience—the two halves of corporate branding. It's clear how important Dave Whitwam has been to Whirlpool's successful corporate branding and growth. He envisioned the Whirlpool of the future, wanted all the world to see it, and made it happen, as he says, "only with the people of Whirlpool."

True direction must come from the top. Especially direction for change. And no change is perhaps as critical today as the move to corporate branding.

The executive with the best opportunity to observe the company from all viewpoints and empowered to make appropriate changes is the CEO. He or she is the one who must have the creativity and foresight to determine where the company should be heading, the communications skill to impart this vision effectively to others, and the power to secure funding to implement whatever changes are required.

In other words, the initial responsibility for successful corporate branding has to be the CEO's alone, even though the organization executes branding and is ultimately responsible for its success or failure. The successful CEO understands his company, its markets, competitors, and investors, and isn't afraid of the challenge of creative change.

Whirlpool had a global view. A leading competitor, Maytag, had a more myopic outlook. At one point, both companies started at the same $2 billion level. But Whirlpool, under visionary leadership and riding a global corporate brand, grew to $6 billion in a couple of years. Over that same period, Maytag stagnated at the $2 billion mark.

LEADING THE CHARGE FOR CHANGE

Donald Bainton, CEO of Continental Can, speaking on the vital subject of change, noted the similarities of his philosophy with that of Whirlpool's Whitwam. "Good management starts with understanding what the business is all about. Too many [executives] tend to see themselves as specialists, [but] there is a continuing responsibility to be well informed with a thorough understanding of the business, its problems and opportunities.

"The second key responsibility is to plan ahead for change. There are very few people who are willing to cause new direction and change. We are creatures of habit, who are most comfortable when our coffee arrives at the same time every morning—when our routines are patterned. Most people feel threatened by change, but the opposite should be true.

"Challenge and change bring out the best that management has to offer. If you are not out there in the lead for change, you are going to be in for some very rough times, because the forces for change at work in the world are massive.

"I am not talking about change to cover up problems, such as reorganization as a veneer for business difficulties. I am talking about changes to turn problems into opportunities. But the truth of the matter is that very few people will take the leadership role to initiate changes to overcome problems."[8]

Unfortunately, the risk-averse includes many chief executive officers. Not all of them, by any means, are like Jack Welch, Dave Whitwam, or Don Bainton. Not all are equipped with enough imagination, spirit, and vision to see the future for their companies. Not all understand the need and can lead the charge for change.

Nor do all even believe in the value of two-way communications, or comprehend the many uses of the communications tools available. They simply do not know how to put these tools to work to bring about the changes necessary to evolve an effective corporate branding program.

In observing why creative change often doesn't take hold in a corporation, it is abundantly apparent just how much influence the top executive can exert. If he or she wants to make something happen, the odds are good that it will happen. If the CEO only pays lip service to meaningful actions, then all he's going to get is lip service. For all the money and effort spent, the CEO will end up with a superficial branding program, nothing more. Employees have an uncanny ability to distinguish whether a change is for real or whether it's only talk.

FALLING FROM GRACE

We began this chapter by discussing the road—or roads—by which today's CEO may reach that much-sought-after pinnacle. I'd like to wind it up with a brief look at at least one way he or she may then "fall from grace."

Murray Hillman, president of the Strategy Workshop, writes in *Advertising Age,* "Corporate America is in deep trouble. We have lost our competitiveness as industry after industry has gone down the tubes, not because advertising lacks creativity or effectiveness, [but] because marketing is lousy. A review of Nielsen data since 1980 indicates that 9 out of 10 new American products—approximately 6,000 each year—failed.

"Did the New Coke launch in 1985 fail because of bad advertising, or because of the marketing blunder of the century? After bringing the original Coke back to the marketplace, the president of Coca-Cola said 'I forgot what kind of love affair America had with the original Coca-Cola brand.' How can any Coke marketing man forget the marketing mission through 100 years of great client marketing and billions of dollars of great consumer advertising: to build a special love affair between the customer and Coca-Cola.

"Companies with the finest laboratories have an even poorer new-product record. In the late `80s Kodak launched five new products—all of which failed. In this case, wiser heads prevailed. The company's board, after years of management neglect, decided to change the CEO responsible for inept marketing rather than change [advertising] agencies.

"The final piece of evidence that supports the proposition that client marketing in America has failed is quite compelling. Chief executives of some of the most prestigious firms are being 'retired' with increasing frequency. However, CEOs in such companies as IBM, Kodak, American Express, General Motors, Westinghouse, and Sears have not been `retired' by friendly outside directors.

"These icons of American business were fired by consumers— more precisely, by consumers they couldn't get with the new-product failures, by quality consumers they couldn't manufacture with creative marketing strategies, by consumers driven away by steady and abusive price increases and, finally, by proprietary customers driven away by yo-yo price promotions.

"In short, CEOs were fired because their in-house marketing strategy and performance failed to create and build consumer demand."[9]

UNLOVED LEADERS

"Corporate America is full of unloved leaders," writes Virginia Munger Kahn in *The New York Times,* "chief executives whose absence makes shareholders' hearts grow fonder.

"When Daniel E. Gill, chairman of Bausch & Lomb, announced his resignation, investors promptly made their pleasure clear. In fact, they judged the company to be worth $150 million more with Mr. Gill gone.

"When Allied Signal replaced Edward L. Hennessy Jr. with Lawrence A. Bossidy, investors added $500 million to the value of the company. For Allied Signal—and three other companies: General Motors, Tenneco, and Goodyear—these one-day bumps added six percent to fifteen percent to the price of their shares."[10]

Generally, the chief executive has more influence over his company's fortunes than anyone else. Thus a leadership change can benefit an enterprise in a number ways; if the chief is jettisoned by the board, for example, it may mean the directors are finally addressing longstanding problems.

This is not to say that changing chief executives assures improved performance. But there is enough history to suggest that in the future the chief executive officer who fails to understand the value of all aspects of marketing and marketing communications— particularly as they apply to corporate branding—is in for a short tenure. Because the CEO who doesn't use communication assets effectively and consistently is likely to be without a vision for his corporation's future and without a plan for corporate growth.

Conversely, it seems clear that the chief executive officer who knows how to communicate and employs corporate brand imaginatively is well positioned to boost stockholder value as well as his or her own.

NOTES

1. Amanda Bennett, "Path to Top Job Now Twists and Turns," *The Wall Street Journal,* March 15, 1993.
2. Robert Lear, *How to Turn Your MBA into a CEO* (Macmillan, 1987).
3. Bennett, "Path to Top Job."
4. "CE Roundtable: CEO's Strategies to Increase Share Price," *Chief Executive,* July/August 1994.
5. Andrew Campbell, "The Power of Mission: Aligning Strategy and Culture," *Planning Review,* Special Issue, September/October 1992.
6. Leonard Saffir, "Would PR Folks Make Good Corporate CEOs?" *Advertising Age,* September 21, 1992.
7. Noel M. Tichy and Stratford Sherman, "Control Your Destiny or Someone Else Will," Doubleday/Currency, 1993, reprinted in *Point of View,* Spencer Stuart Executive Search Consultants, Winter 1993.
8. Donald Bainton, speech given at C. W. Post School of Business, November 12, 1992.
9. Murray Hillman, "CEOs: Look at Your Record before Firing the Ad Agency," *Advertising Age.*
10. Virginia Munger Kahn, "If the Boss Walks Out the Door, Investors May Rush In," *The New York Times,* January 7, 1996.

CHAPTER FIFTEEN

TWO SOURCES OF AID FOR THE CEO

*"Despite their ultimate authority over company manage-
ment, corporate boards of directors have long been accused
of giving executives free rein to take companies where they
wanted. While such rubber-stamp boards no doubt still
exist, the new danger may not be sleepy boards but
hyperactive ones."*[1]

　　—THOMAS A. COLE
　　THE NEW YORK TIMES

We have seen that the successful chief executive officer must fully
understand and be able to employ the various aspects of corporate
communications. He or she has a vision for the company, but must
be able to articulate that vision, clearly and persuasively, to the
company's own people and to the financial community. And the
CEO must be sure the corporate brand reflects that vision.

This is a broad task and not an easy one. Communications, as
vital as they are, are not the CEO's only responsibility, and in fact,
may not even be considered the top priority by some CEOs. There is
help, however, for the CEO who seeks it. This chapter investigates
two valuable sources for that aid, the first being the company's
board of directors, especially the external members.

The role of corporate boards of directors has been in continuous
flux, energized by the turbulent economic, political, social, technological, and environmental context in which today's corporate
enterprise must now be governed.

This change is the result of a number of forces. Says Cole, "One is shareholder activism and the scrutiny of corporate governance it inspires. Another is a pair of takeover cases, [with the resulting] message for directors clear: Don't take your duties for granted. Faced with these developments, directors demanded and thoroughly probed information. They learned to act as actual decision makers.

"But whatever the sources of director activism, many chief executives believe it will only grow. According to a survey . . . 82 percent of top executives believe boards will become 'increasingly critical of management performance.'"[2]

A 1995 study, conducted jointly by the National Association of Corporate Directors and Deloitte & Touche LLP, reveals that companies are heeding the suggestions of investor activists, academics, and corporate consultants by strengthening governance practices and moving to smaller, more independent boards.

Update comments, "Shareholder activism is moving to the next level, with two major objectives: direct influence with top management and the board to bring about change in companies; and increasing authority of boards while making them more responsive to shareholders.

"Institutional activists are determined to make directors use their authority in managing management, shaping strategy and achieving satisfactory investment returns. . . . Board composition is changing. More companies have a majority of outside directors [and] are putting only outside directors on their board committees. . . . and are looking to find needed expertise in improving performance."[3]

Not only has investor relations come into the boardroom, but it's a trend that requires board members to fully understand just how their companies are viewed by the investment community. The result is that more and more companies now make regular presentations to their boards, with investor relations people playing important roles in these meetings. These presentations generally include insights into why a company is perceived the way it is and why stock price is rising or falling.

Now better informed on investor behavior and stock performance, directors are being told to carefully evaluate management's ability to deliver results. When investment returns are seen as unsatisfactory, directors are expected to force change.

THE BOARD AND THE BRAND

A case in point: When outside directors on the board of General Motors pressed for and received the resignation of the chairman and chief executive officer, Robert C. Stempel, they caused reverberations in boardrooms across the country.

At the time, Alison Leigh Cowan commented in *The New York Times*, "the awakening of the once sleepy G.M. board will redefine the cozy relationship that often exists between the nation's top executives and the hand-picked members of their boards. . . . From now on the acceptable conduct of outside directors is to take an independent view of the way management is dealing with sensitive problems and to require a sense of urgency in dealing with them.

"The ensuing uproar and political pressure helped the Securities and Exchange Commission enact reforms giving shareholders greater power to force change at underperforming companies. Directors are injecting a new sense of urgency into the boardroom, letting chief executives know in no uncertain terms that poor performance will result in dismissal."[4]

What does this have to do with a corporation's vision and its motivation to create and employ a meaningful corporate brand? Much.

Boards now look for clear communication from the CEO to the company's key publics. Experienced directors understand that communications is one of the most powerful weapons in the CEO's arsenal. Knowing when and how to use it is viewed as an indispensable leadership attribute in a current or potential chief executive officer.

EVALUATING THE BOARD

Writes Robert K. Mueller, "In evaluating a board and an individual director's effectiveness, two basic questions must be answered: How well is the board of directors relating to current needs of the company? How well does the board deal with the futurity of current business decisions?"[5]

According to Mueller there are several evaluative criteria that indicate the effectiveness of directors in meeting present and future needs:

- "The commitment and interest of individual directors. The time is past when the purpose of being on a board is to be a member of the 'club.' A deep interest and commitment to the company are a primary requirement."

- "Competence as related to the needs of the corporation.

Boards need members with business and professional know-how pertinent to the corporation's activities."

- "General functional strength of individual directors. Boards need members with basic functional talents to provide imaginative guidance and aid in such major areas as general management, strategic planning, social and political policy, finance, and international affairs."

And perhaps most relevant of all:

- "The director's role as a change agent. Boards can exercise the role of change agent for the enterprise. This role differs from the traditional judicial performance of making go or no-go decisions on management proposals. A board can develop ideas of its own. But this requires an atmosphere conducive to change and individual board members able and willing to suggest going beyond traditional evaluative or judicial processes. Imagination, innovation, and willingness to suggest trying new concepts and ideas are attributes vitally needed in many boardrooms."

A Competent Sounding Board

Is it the board's specific responsibility to create the corporate brand? No, of course not. But a board can act as a sounding board for major corporate communications going out from the CEO—from brand advertising to corporate advertising, from public relations to investor to employee relations, and everything in between. And these communications should be consistent. In fact, the board must demand consistency in this respect from the CEO.

Without consistency, there can be no effective corporate brand. It is incumbent upon each board member to clearly understand that there is not just one measure of corporate success. There are many measures and certainly market share and customer allegiance are high on the list. Both are directly influenced by corporate branding, and so it becomes a "must" that board members seek consistent communications from the CEO as prerequisite to a working corporate branding program.

Oftentimes the CEO is so tied up with day-to-day business that he or she loses sight of one of the position's most important responsibilities: the care and nuturing of the corporate brand. He either neglects the task or assigns it to someone who does not have the

CEO's authority to articulate the vision for the company, or the power to push a branding program through and maintain it adequately.

The board of directors needs to carefully monitor the corporate persona. They need to say to the CEO: "We don't believe the company's image is what it should be. We should be able to evaluate our image in some sort of systematic way. How do we stack up against our peer groups?" Coming from the outside they have a better perspective and can give the CEO the kind of endorsement that says: "It's all right to pay attention to image. Don't worry, it's not just your responsibility, but ours too. Together we can make it work."

Sometimes a CEO just doesn't have the training or background to fully appreciate the value of corporate image, and needs the support and suggestions that come from the board's broader experience.

LEVERAGE THE "BEST THINGS"

Thomas Keeton, former Director of Advertising for Lockheed (now Lockheed-Martin), says that the chairman always sets the tone for corporate communications. His statement is always that our first job is to build the best possible product; the second job is to deliver it at an affordable price; and the third, to communicate the best things about our company. We must leverage our reputation as far as it can go. So you see, he recognizes the need for communications.

"After you've built a good product and delivered it at an affordable price, the thing to do is to leverage those facts to a higher level so that you can obtain maximum possible benefit from doing it. This is the nub of corporate branding. It's fine to say that if you build a better mousetrap the world will beat a path to your door. But they won't if they don't know about it."

That's one side of the coin, with a board and board chairman who understand their particular role and responsibility in today's corporate structure.

But, unfortunately, there are not enough boards who think like that. According to Alex A. Meyer, himself a former chairman and board member for several leading corporations, "Many board members, through no fault of their own, do not really understand corporate brand advertising and its value. Very few understand the residual value of corporate brand advertising and its lasting effects.

"This is not meant as criticism, but some board members have just not been with companies that have brands conducive to corporate brand advertising. Or, in some cases, short term bottom line demands curtail corporate brand advertising. In others, lack of strategic planning or just plain short-sightedness is the reason. Although print advertising, television commercials, etc. may be reviewed periodically at the board level, corporate brand advertising is seldom discussed."

On Ceding Stewardship of the Brand

Can board involvement have a negative effect on corporate branding? For example, what can happen if the CEO abdicates his responsibility to the process? Can a board member then go too far—wield too much influence on the corporate brand? Indeed, yes! And a board member may thus do a decided disservice to the company.

I know of a certain software company that sought to change its name and corporate brand. They had no specific plan, however, to analyze, create, and implement the change.

This company had a strong external board member who happened to have good credentials in consumer advertising. He greatly impressed the other directors, especially the CEO, with his capabilities. As a result, and ignoring obvious internal company assets, the CEO abdicated his own responsibility as the company's number one communicator, leaving the project for the director to handle. In effect, an outside board member became the ultimate decision maker on many aspects of the program.

Unfortunately, and despite his advertising background, the board member treated this emerging software company as if it were a large consumer account. He spent a lot of time and many precious dollars to produce only mediocre work. Results might have been more on target—and less costly—with a carefully thought out corporate branding program.

It was a case of a member of the board abusing his role, satisfying his own personal ego. But even more to the point, it was a case of a CEO backing away from his responsibility, turning authority over to an "outsider," while ignoring the professional, objective point of view of marketing, advertising, and PR counsel.

This, of course, is only an anecdotal example. If anything, it only proves that a CEO must maintain full control if he or she is to give the company a meaningful corporate brand. The board and its individual members can be highly useful, but should never take the place of the CEO. Despite whatever help he may require, the weight of the corporate branding program must remain on the CEO's shoulders.

A Climate That Supports the Brand

Corporate branding is not a hit or miss project. It is a long term plan and commitment and/or strategy, requiring a real investment in time and money. Some board members are willing to make this investment, but many are not. When they are, however, and when wisely utilized, they can offer unmatched assistance to a busy CEO.

The power to improve the performance of a corporate board usually resides pretty much within the board itself. Up to now, there has been little incentive for boards to address questions regarding their own operations because few shareholders saw a connection between the excellence of board processes and corporate results. However, a board's efforts to improve these processes can yield important results. For one thing they can foster a climate that supports, enables, and ultimately demands the full achievement of business potential. And naturally this includes the establishment of a carefully planned corporate branding program.

The CEO must lead the way. He or she has to propose a plan with specific goals, to be implemented over an extended period of time, and must put forth the necessary corporate communications to activate the branding program and achieve the goals. It should go without saying that the CEO must also make sure that each and every board member understands the message communicated and is in full agreement and support.

Once done, the board can play an active and helpful role in the branding process. The members' various backgrounds and expertise should prove invaluable to the CEO and to the ultimate success of the corporate brand and its contribution to the future of the corporation.

A New Kind of Senior Officer

The second potential source of assistance to the CEO in the creation and maintenance of a corporate brand comes from an area that actually doesn't exist today in most companies. I'm referring to the establishment of a new kind of corporate senior officer, a CCO or chief communications officer. Let's see why.

Throughout this book, we have stressed the role of corporate communications as the major responsibility of the chief executive officer. It is the CEO who has the experience, the leadership, the understanding and focus on *all* business facets of the company. It is the CEO who has the vision of where his company is going and how it is going to get there.

But the CEO, by anyone's definition, is a busy person, with many responsibilities in a wide variety of activities. So often tied up with day-to-day business, the CEO may easily lose sight of one of his major assignments: the care and feeding of the corporate brand.

Furthermore, he or she may not have the background necessary for the smooth, effective communication of ideas and plans for corporate branding. Because primary experience may have been in areas such as finance, engineering, or production, the CEO's training may not have fully emphasized the values of corporate communications and of corporate branding in particular.

Whatever his or her past exposure, however, the CEO is under pressure all the time. And as important to a company's performance as corporate branding may be, the CEO can be under such pressure from other sectors that the corporate brand will get little if any of his attention. As a result, corporate communications will often end up taking a back seat to other company advertising and public relations.

That a CEO may be too pressed to attend effectively to other responsibilities may be reasonably certain. But in many cases he is given able and experienced support in the form of a chief financial officer (CFO), chief operations officer (COO), chief administrative officer (CAO), or whatever.

Only in the all-important area of corporate communications is this assistance overlooked. So why not create a chief communications officer, a CCO, reporting directly to the CEO?

The Corporate Advertising Practices Study

In the Association of National Advertisers' 1994 Corporate Advertising Practices study, we posed the question, "There are Chief Financial Officers and Chief Information Officers. What about a 'Chief Communications Officer?'"

The responses were highly encouraging. As many as 64 percent of respondents believed it would be helpful for the corporation to have a CCO. Only 16 percent felt that it wouldn't. The balance had not made up their minds.

The question "What role would you envision a 'Chief Communications Officer' playing in your company?" provoked a lot of serious thinking on the subject. Here are verbatim responses representing a good cross-section:

- Oversee the vision, development, and monitoring of all internal and external communications.

- Integrate a common communications platform across all units and all media and all audiences.
- As a valued, empowered executive, the CCO would drive all communications on the brand toward one cohesive, unified positioning.
- Develop an overall communications strategy that would encompass corporate and line businesses. Provide intellectual leadership in the demanding area of communications. Set communications standards and policies.
- Ensure synergy between advertising and public affairs and between advertising campaigns.
- Strategic direction of all internal/external communications. Oversight of communications activity worldwide.
- Member of management board—advises senior management on communications implications of company strategies/decisions, etc.
- Champion of the brand in all communications—the focal point for all divisions of the company—to help each leverage the brand to the benefit of specific divisions and the cumulative benefit of the brand.

PUT THE VISION TO WORK

The CEO may have the vision, but often will not have the time to execute it. Nor should he have to. But without someone in the company positioned high enough up and able to support that vision constantly, guarding it jealously, the CEO's direction for the future easily becomes watered down. Worse, it may become the object of attack by various cliques and power bases within the corporation.

A CCO, there to oversee that vision, would nurture it and promulgate it to the world. In effect, the CCO would make sure that the CEO's vision for the company is effectively and dynamically put to work.

The CEO would certainly see to it that an appropriate corporate brand, based on the CEO's vision, is established and integrated into all corporate communications, both external and internal. Properly executed, such a common communications platform can only bring extra value to the company.

Ranked on a plane with the CFO and COO, the CCO would be given the necessary clout to say to the various advertising, promotion, public, employee, and investor relations factions within the company, "Let's work together to accomplish a specific goal." And he would be able to make sure that it happened.

There will be CEOs, of course, who neither want nor feel they need such assistance. Rightly or wrongly, they may believe that they are completely capable of addressing such matters as corporate communications and corporate branding without the "interference" of the board and without the necessity of adding one more senior officer to the team.

There are indeed such independent, strong-willed, creative, and articulate chief executive officers. But not all that many of them. But for those who aren't—and recognize this truth—we strongly suggest that they consider at least one of my two proposals. There are sure to be external board members whose experience as successful communicators could be put to good use. And the addition of a CCO, a professional corporate communicator who has senior-level responsibilities as a policymaker, could provide the necessary leadership.

NOTES

1. Thomas A. Cole, "Drawing the Line on Corporate Boards," *The New York Times,* January 16, 1994.
2. Ibid.
3. "Activism Is Making Strong Headway," *Update,* September 1994, National Investor Relations Institute.
4. Alison Leigh Cowan, "The High-Energy Board Room," *The New York Times,* October 28, 1992.
5. "Boardworthiness/From a President's and a Director's Perspective," Robert K. Mueller, American Management Association, 1994.

LEVI STRAUSS AND CO.: "ONE OF THE GREAT GLOBAL BRANDS"

A conversation between the author and John Onoda, vice president—corporate communications at Levi Strauss & Co. (LS & Co.), regarding the building and maintaining of the company's corporate brand.

During the Gold Rush that began in 1849, one merchant who saw an opportunity was Levi Strauss. He manufactured bib-less blue denim overalls, reinforced at points of stress with copper rivets. These were exceedingly popular with the workers in the American West. In time the trademark Levis became a synonym for blue denim pants, and the name has continued on and now is known and respected around the world.

Gregory: Can you give me an overview of your corporate image policies and issues?

Onoda: Levi Strauss & Co. is privately held. We have a tradition going back over a century of a strong orientation toward values, strong support of the community, and an excellent product—a lot of the fundamental elements of corporate brand, and what today is called corporate reputation. It didn't have a name way back when.

Today, we're probably in a unique position worldwide as one of the handful of great global brands, up there with McDonald's, Coca-Cola, Sony, and a few others. We may possibly have put more energy into defining and instituting our corporate values

EXHIBIT A   LEVI'S TRADEMARK LOGO

than any of the others. Ours is a progressive, liberal sort of company; most of them are conservative.

Historically, we have had an unusual set of philanthropic activity guidelines, where we regularly made contributions to the communities where we did business but were forbidden from seeking publicity about it. And this historic approach filtered into the company's philosophy about corporate reputational management. A word of mouth reputation has developed over generations that this company cares about communities. We do things like helping to build schools of business, museums, or what have you, or create entire philanthropic organizations. As individuals, the major shareholders have grown up in an environment of high reputation and have maintained it through deeds, not words. They have been conscientiously avoiding the limelight.

Levi Strauss & Co. has had a very interesting way of creating a corporate reputation. We seek to change the business to address the issues, but we haven't done much chest thumping. We hope that eventually word of mouth will promulgate the message. So the way LS & Co. would address the environmental issue is to put together a global task force, decide what we can do to change our business practices and those of our contractors, and then take a leadership position in environmental management. The last thing we might think of, or get around to, is the marketing element. That's the difference between reputation and image. You can create an image. Simply throw enough money at it and run some super advertising, and you can create an image. The danger is the gap between the image and the reality. All companies and organizations have to deal with that gap The standards which we hold may seem unrealistic, and we'd rather not have publicity about them. So we try to do the substantive work and let that speak for itself, building our long-term reputation on the deeds. It may cost us money. It will cost us time. It could cost us markets, but if you're in it for another century, or another 140 years, we believe that this is the proper approach. Two generations from now you'll know who played the hand better!

Gregory: How do you feel that helps the company long term?

Onoda: Let's take an example. The company recently established a business in India. If you're following what's going on there, most Western companies have tremendous problems with intellectual property rights, bureaucratic hurdles, and the like. Historically, it's been a very challenging place for Western companies to do business. Let's assume there are several jeans companies trying to get in. We don't simply put up billboards with a bunch of people of different colors. We go in and say we have a history of respecting diversity, that we have a company filled with local people who are truly empowered and who broaden the organization's perspective.

We have a history of contributing to the community, involving the employees, giving them funds and letting them have time off from work for community involvement. It goes back generations. We respect people of all backgrounds and colors. We integrated our plants in the U.S. South before civil rights legislation.

We're not reciting marketing slogans; we're telling our history. Other companies might come in and say, "Gee! We have these billboards, and look, we have this rainbow coalition on the billboards." That's image. But we have substance going back decades. Now who do you think the government is going to give the permit to? Who do you think the best contractors are going to want to work for? And that's a business advantage, because there's only a finite number of best business partners or government permits that are going to be issued. India is a market with 200 million people in the middle class alone. We're going to do well in this market, in part because of our corporate reputation.

This is our model. This is the Levi Strauss model.

Gregory: How do you measure its success?

Onoda: Over the past decade, we've seen our sales, earnings, brand reputation, and corporate reputation all build rapidly. Compared to the Fortune 500 in terms of profitability over the last decade, Levi Strauss & Co. belongs near the very top. The company has doubled in size in the last eight years alone. Look at other measurements, like the quality of the workforce or quality of management. I'm sure you've been inside enough major organizations to know that quality of people is a very powerful element in determining a company's success.

Take myself, for example. I've headed up communications groups or departments here, at McDonald's, and at the Holiday Corporation, which formerly owned Holiday Inns and still holds Harrah's Casinos. So I've been in the guts of three global megabrands. Naturally I have received resumes—job applications—at all three places, but never the number I've gotten here. Part of it is because of our San Francisco location. But I'm getting resumes from people who say, "I'm incredibly successful in my career, but it's meaningless. I hate the company I work for. I hate the agency. It's just work and my professional life has no meaning. I want more out of it."

I've never found that anywhere else, and I hear my counterparts in other departments throughout this organization have the same thing happening to them. Part of it may be our location in the Bay area, but a lot of it is the company's reputation. It's phenomenal.

Gregory: While I was sitting outside, a lady came in and chatted with the receptionist for a few minutes. She said, "Can you believe Lisa is leaving the company?" She went on to say, "This is the greatest company in the world to work for. How could anybody leave?"

Onoda: Our voluntary turnover is extraordinarily low. Why? Because ours is a company of substance, where values and people are truly respected. This ties back to a substantive reputation as opposed to marketing reputation. There's more here than meets the eye.

Gregory: As good as it sounds, I believe it's a very difficult formula for most companies to follow.

Onoda: That's right. We're privately held by the same family. It's a unique set of circumstances, and I'm not sure it can be duplicated. For example, we are asked to act in accordance with our values, so we screen for values-driven individuals. Our compensation is directly tied to behaviors relating to ethics, respect for diversity, empowerment, and so on. And we attract people who are excited by that kind of environment, who want to live that way. Worldwide, we attract them.

Gregory: And you find them by ads, by word of mouth?

Onoda: We'll take out ads, but if you see our ad, it won't just say in tiny print, "Equal Employment Opportunity." It will say proudly "we're especially eager for diversity so come and join us." But mostly it's word of mouth.

Gregory: So you have an infrastructure in place that supports the values?

Onoda: Absolutely. Our training is unique. Salaried professionals are out for a week of leadership training, off-site with a bunch of colleagues, about 20 people from around the world. It's another four days for diversity and ethics training. It includes the study of an ethical principle, decision-making model that teaches how to do a stakeholder analysis.

The kicker is that all of these activities, from morning to night when they are off-site, have a senior manager leading the session. And he or she could be the chairman or president, or head of one of our major businesses or departments. And they're not just there to say "welcome," disappear, and then show up at the end to hand you a diploma. He or she is there on site as an instructor, from breakfast in the morning to dancing and beers at night.

We all do it. I do it and the chairman does it every year. The learning for us is tremendous. You don't discover that much if you just deliver a pep talk and hand out diplomas. But if you're going through physical activities and tough small group discussions, trying to coach and answer questions on the spur of the moment, that's tremendously different.

Ours is such a different culture; it's like entering a different universe. As it is now, everyone comes in through a different door, with a different set of experiences. We try to guide them to the same point, but they go at different paces and get different messages. It's very confusing. It really takes years. And we weed out a lot of people who don't make it on the cultural level. The professional stuff is relatively easy for us.

We're a world-class brand and can pay good money in San Francisco for a top accountant, a top communicator, a top lawyer. But finding someone who can make that cultural journey is tremendously difficult.

Gregory: That's highly interesting.

Onoda: Let me bring us back to earth. This is our model, not an advertising model but a corporate reputation model. We define corporate reputation as a global asset. Why? Because everyone in the company has responsibility for it. Financial performance is included as one of the components. So if you come to work and do well and help us make a profit, you are contributing to the asset. Conversely, if you call a news reporter and say that this place is full of swindlers and jerks, you diminish the asset.

So, it's a unique asset. Every employee has some responsibility and some accountability for this asset. It's different from advertising in terms of how you manage it. Advertising goes straight to the consumer; then they buy the product and have an experience with the product. With corporate reputation you go to the suppliers, the customers, the employees, etc. You generate word of mouth, very often indirectly, and then maybe that will translate into a buying position at the point of sale. But it's the exact opposite of advertising; you don't aim directly at the point of sale. You aim at the other end of the business process chain.

Corporate reputation is pretty much based on perception, how you are perceived by different stakeholder audiences. You have to know what the key audiences are, and we identified them. To Levi Strauss & Co., the major elements of a corporate reputation are products, services, financial performance, quality management, marketing activity, workplace policies, and corporate citizenship.

Different stakeholder groups, in different communities, will put different emphasis on those of these they draw upon to develop their own feeling of corporate reputation.

Gregory: So there might be more emphasis on one component than another?

Onoda: Exactly. Banks and financial organizations would look at financial performance. For nongovernmental organizations it could be workplace practices and corporate citizenship. Consumers in developing countries might be more interested in the quality of products and services. For the media, of course, marketing activity will be disproportionately impactful.

After a lot of work, we narrowed it down to this cluster. These are things we can influence directly. So how do you go about it? For us it's a matter of doing a global grid and saying here is the grab bag of corporate reputation elements. Who are the local audiences? Is it a highly developed nation, an urban market, a non-urban market? What do they value? We believe it's a global village, and we can't afford to have inconsistent messages anywhere in the world.

Gregory: That's well thought out. Your advertising—your brand advertising—how do you incorporate these values into that?

Onoda: You know, we don't do cause-related marketing without a lot of thought about its fit with our corporate culture and values, as well as our long term business objectives. We won't thump our chests with press releases until we've invested countless manhours and millions of dollars to make the substance a reality. Our concern is always to do all the substantive things first. Recycle our denim scraps, be in compliance with the laws of every country where we work, ensure that our contractors are in compliance with the laws of the environment, and then tie environmental issues to external communications.

We were the preeminent company in terms of AIDS education. We received the Harvard Dively Award for our leadership in this area. We were keynote speaker at the U.S. AIDS Conference. And our president of international operations resigned to become one of the leaders in the AIDS education community. If any company has impeccable credentials concerning AIDS education in the workplace, we do. And we have the programs, policies, groups, and history to show it. The reality does match whatever public relations stance we might take. If we start getting into other areas, we will have similar substance behind public relations and marketing initiatives.

Gregory: But does your brand advertising relate to values at all, or is it totally separate?

Onoda: It's not totally separate. For one thing, we have such a dense corporate culture. Take, for example, our respect for diversity. If you look at our women's advertising—which has won us tremendous amounts of kudos—we don't feature "bimbos in bustiers." Instead, we've done these Matisse-like cartoons that talk about a woman's inner feelings. They simply show a woman's shape as opposed to a model's, which is a shape that 99 percent of the women can't really achieve. This is because we respect diversity. We wouldn't want to get into that sort of stereotyping.

Our advertising and marketing are consistent with our culture. But do we try to include all the components of our culture in them? No, I wouldn't say that. I don't believe we would try to market ethical behavior, for example. Diversity, something we're so sensitive to being in San Francisco's melting pot, is a lot easier. Look at our ads; you'll see tremendous diversity. Or merely walk our hallways.

There's a business payoff in this that's exponentially greater than what you'd get out of a short-term investment in bill-boards. If you're willing to go through all this effort and truly build this sort of organization, then you build an organization that has the best people, the best partners, the best financial performance, and almost no turnover unless you want it.

Gregory: A number of years ago we helped reposition a major cor-poration in the mind of the public, taking them from very quiet philanthropic activity to the point of asking for some recognition for what they had been doing. It worked well, and I have to counsel clients who spend money on philanthropic endeavors without any benefit, that there is no return on that.

Onoda: I agree with you entirely. The first major disagreement I had with the chairman when I took this job was concerning the flat-out prohibition of any kind of publicity about the company's philanthropic activities. That was the first policy I worked to reverse.

But there are no models for us. We are the model for other companies. It's exciting because we have great freedom, and a great sense of adventure and risk taking. It's also slow and dif-ficult.

Gregory: I think a lot of companies hedge their image with the finan-cial community. They want to look like a good company, a good corporate citizen, and so they do things—things that are not really true to the soul of the company.

Onoda: And not really consistent, either. We're doing a better job than most companies in this regard. I could take you through the entire company on a global basis and show you a hundred examples of how everyone—not just the chairman—respects and acts upon our corporate values. It's holistic throughout our organization.

Currently, I'm working on employee performance reviews. All of the company's salaried employees worldwide have 360-degree assessments based on inputs from a sampling of all the people they work with. Secretaries provide input on profession-als. Even clients and outside people are asked for performance feedback. I have my PR agency evaluate me, and others in my department make the same choice. I don't think there's another communications department in the world where you would ask outside vendors to provide comments that would influence your compensation.

But one element of the company's business vision is to be the "Customer of Choice." What this means is that even if we weren't this great global brand, even if we didn't pay our bills on time, suppliers would want to work on our account. That's because we're the sort of people with whom they are excited to work, the sort who give them opportunities they can't have anywhere else. We don't go around promoting this, but word gets out. Don't you think that if you were a PR agency and knew you could have this kind of relationship, you would want to work with us? What's that worth?

Gregory: Isn't your chairman actually part of the Strauss family?

Onoda: Bob Haas is the great-great grandnephew of Levi Strauss, and quite a guy.

Gregory: And visionary?

Onoda: More visionary that any other chairman I have ever met or heard of.

Gregory: That's rare in a family business, a privately held business.

Onoda: It may be unique, but all I know is that it's working. A lot of companies could not do what we do, even if they wanted to, especially those that are publicly held. There are too many external forces, from Wall Street and other quarters. But we can do it here, and our feeling is, well, why not try?

Gregory: What would you recommend for a smaller company? One that's been struggling with things like, what should our values be? That type of thing.

Onoda: They can study companies such as our own and Herman Miller. The literature is out there. The trick is to really take it seriously. It's incredibly dense, as dense as creating a new culture on the planet.

Gregory: A couple of companies have really integrated quality into their systems and become different companies.

Onoda: I'm not saying that we don't have all the acronyms for quality here. But it all comes down to good management. After the acronyms are gone, we're still going to be quality driven. We're still going to be reengineering. We're still going to be a learning organization. To us, that's just good management.

Gregory: Very good. And thank you.

No company has embraced a values-based strategy the way Levi Strauss & Co. has. Says Chairman and CEO Robert D. Haas, the great-great grandnephew of founder Levi Strauss, "We are not doing this because it makes us feel good—although it does. We are not doing this because it is politically correct. We are doing this because we believe in the interconnection between liberating the talents of our people and business success."[1]

NOTE

1. Russell Mitchell and Michael O'Neal, "Managing By Values," *Business Week,* August 1, 1994.

HANCOR, INC.: THE CRITICAL PATH TO STARTING A CORPORATE BRANDING PROGRAM

This is a step-by-step case history of one company that did it right—that recognized its need for corporate branding and took the necessary actions to achieve it— truly a textbook case. What's more, it's a study of a company that both small, entrepreneurial companies and larger enterprises can relate to. It was a true team effort between Corporate Branding Partnership and our client, and it worked extremely well.

What was the key to the program's success? For starters, we had permission from a committed, articulate, and visioned management to do it all the right way. Management understood the time it takes to review all data, and they worked closely with us to fill in the blanks with targeted research to both external and internal audiences. We were able to identify all key components of the infrastructure. Everything fell into proper place.

This client possessed an unusually open management philosophy. It was a management with a clear vision of where they wanted to take the company—a vision which they could fully articulate. And it was a vision with which we concurred, one we knew was attainable.

The client also recognized and understood the importance of corporate branding throughout the organization at all levels, with the corporate brand integrated into all communications, internal as well as external.

Management knew that all employees can be a meaningful part of the process, and that they have their own valuable input for the corporate brand. Astutely, they wanted each and every employee to understand what was going on in the company, and why. In our mind this is integral to how corporate branding should work ideally.

The company could supply us with a wealth of information about their own business and their industry in general. Working together with them as a team, we would combine this insight into their marketplace with current market trends, market history, and competitive activity, and we could assist them in improving their corporate brand.

BACKGROUND

Hancor Inc., headquartered in Findlay, Ohio, has annual sales in excess of $150 million, primarily in corrugated polyethylene (PE) pipe, and has been producing quality drainage products for well over a century. In the 1960s, the company implemented a major technology shift. Highly durable plastics were then being developed, with plastic pipe already achieving acceptance in Europe and Japan.

Quickly recognizing the opportunity, Hancor rose to the challenge. Their engineers went to work, designing and building the processing equipment and manufacturing plants needed to produce durable polyethylene drainage pipe. In just five years Hancor became an important pioneer in this new and growing field, and today they are a major producer of PE drainage pipe. The company's ongoing commitment to innovation has resulted in a host of products to meet diverse and changing customer needs, including a continual flow of new solutions for storm water problems. Delivering better performance than concrete or metal pipe, Hancor's PE pipe boasts many highly promotable advantages.

To provide the storm water drainage market with superior hydraulics, the company developed Hancor Hi-Q® pipe with its smooth, faster flow-through interior. Then, in 1994 they introduced Hancor Hi-Q.® Sure-Lok™ pipe, engineered with a unique snap-together integral-bell design for water- and silt-tight joints and easy, lightweight installation.

Hancor competes in the drainage market—traditionally a marketplace with a loyal customer base—with an excellent product line, black corrugated polyethylene pipe, although a line generally viewed as generic. Hancor looked to enter new and more competitive markets (storm water, home centers, etc.), and they recognized the need to place more emphasis on their corporate brand. The goal was to create a new image for their particular black PE pipe, an image that would say: "If you're going to buy this kind of product, Hancor is the one to buy"—an image that is particularly desirable in a marketplace with few major competitors.

In addition, as an industry leader they felt the need to correct a perceived lack of marketplace awareness for polyethylene pipe, to promote an appreciation for its many benefits, and to combat certain negative attitudes about plastic pipe in general.

As a major manufacturer of PE pipe—and heading for the leadership position in sales—Hancor is committed to educating target audiences through seminars, videotapes, PR releases, and like techniques as to PE's merits and economies. Key among their constituencies are not only the municipal and other government officials who approve and spec major water drainage projects, but also the engineers and contractors so critical to the Hancor product's actual selection and use.

ESTABLISHING A COMPANY PROFILE

To assist in the development of Hancor's corporate branding program, Corporate Branding Partnership was called in as consultant. Our initial meeting with Hancor's senior management team lasted a day, and we gained many important insights into the company and its industry from Fred Kremer, Jr., president and CEO, and his executive staff.

Hancor understood that the creation and implementation of a corporate brand is not an overnight process. It usually requires about twelve months to get a program up to a full head of steam and as much as three years to gain its full benefit. The process starts and ends with research, while in between are business analysis, strategic planning and communications planning. In the case of Hancor, we would begin by thoroughly studying its heritage, the personality of the company, and its vision for the future.

After the initial meeting, we conducted individual interviews with the management team and a number of Hancor employees. We call this "taking the temperature." We believe employees, the core of an organization, understand what is really happening with the company, and provide a unique and generally accurate perspective. They often have great ideas for improvements and always appreciate being asked their opinions. Employees can be the best spokespeople for a company.

Hancor executives also visited our offices in Stamford, Connecticut, where we conducted in-depth strategy sessions, discussing such subjects as sales and distribution patterns, customer sales and service methods, human resource training programs, and many more. This background would help us better understand the company and its point of view, and aid us in integrating the corporate brand throughout Hancor's internal and external communications.

After studying thoroughly the company's strategies and vision for the future, its value system and culture, we were able to begin the creation of a new logo and nomenclature that would depict Hancor accurately. Their management realized that to obtain the full benefit of corporate branding, the project would be considerably larger than merely arriving at a new symbol and nomenclature. A complete and fully integrated corporate branding campaign would help them up front in every aspect of their sales and marketing, toward the industry leadership desired.

Working hand in hand with Hancor management, we prepared a working schedule, called a critical path, which established guidelines for implementing the project from the ground up as well as from the top down. In conjunction with the goals decided upon, Hancor hoped to get everyone in the company energized around the concept at the very beginning.

At management's recommendation, we interviewed a cross-section of the employees. It should go without saying that you can get a great deal of good input from employees, no matter whether they are managers, production line workers, sales people, or truck drivers. They are the ones most familiar with the issues that affect their individual jobs, and we had to get as close to those issues as possible. We particularly wanted Hancor people to understand that their roles are extremely important to the company.

We went to numerous plant locations across the country and held cross-functional meetings with groups of eight to ten people each. Some of the questions we asked were: What do you believe the image is of Hancor today? What would you like the image to be? How do you think customers perceive us in the marketplace? What would you like customers to say about us? What are the strengths and weaknesses of the company as to growth? How can Hancor increase productivity and profitability?

These questions opened up many other pertinent areas for discussion. Feedback was incredible, and we learned much about Hancor, storm water management, and drainage systems. We also came away with an excellent feeling about the company. Despite a few isolated complaints, we found a deep sense of commitment, dedication, and loyalty among employees. A sense of purpose and real pride. We heard many comments such as "This is my company," "I feel I'm a real part of it," and "This is a solid company to work for."

Many had constructive suggestions as to how the company might improve. It was evident that these employees were totally energized. They enjoyed working for Hancor and wanted the company to move forward quickly to put a real mark on the polyethylene pipe industry. They truly wanted to make their company better. Our mission was to interpret that sense of purpose into an actionable corporate brand.

We prepared and submitted a report on our employee interviews. Then we interviewed a number of Hancor's customers and distributors, as well as engineers and customers, in a series of focus groups. We learned in particular that Hancor was in very good shape with its customers. On the whole they felt that Hancor was the best of the three or four major suppliers of PE drainage pipe with which to do business.

Those studies developed other useful input too, including basic data on the state of the industry, views on pipe properties, decision factors in selecting pipe, reasons for resistance to the use of PE, and familiarity with Hancor.

Combined, all our input from management, employees, customers, distributors, engineers, and contractors gave us a detailed and invaluable profile of both Hancor and its industry.

Developing a Brand Communications Program

At Hancor's request, we started work on the new logo as the first element in a complete, new, and integrated communications program. We came up with a design that we feel truly expresses the spirit of the company, the quality of the product, and the enthusiasm of the management team and employees. We recommended a strong icon, inspired by the product itself with its series of annular, corrugated rings. Hancor was presented with about twenty variations on this theme and finally settled on one, feeling it best reinforces the image of forward, progressive thinking.

We also came up with an appropriate tag line. We zeroed in on "Technology. Innovation. Solutions." giving the line an italic typographic treatment to convey a sense of Hancor's strength and forward movement. Proactive and strategically driven, the line captures the core values of the company. It grew out of management's own feelings and strongly reflects what the Hancor image should involve in the future.

We worked together with Hancor to test the new logo and tag line with various customers and employee groups for their reactions. Response was highly positive and encouraging. The messages in this logo and tag line are both powerful and long lasting. They are a most visible expression of Hancor's mission and commitment to excellence and represent a major step toward communicating clear market leadership for Hancor.

With both logo and tag line approved, the next move was to launch Hancor's corporate communications program. The primary advertising objective was to encourage prospects and specifiers to recognize Hancor as an important supplier of storm water drainage products, offering innovative, market-driven solutions based on state-of-the-art technologies. Potential customers would also be motivated to learn more about how Hancor and its products can help improve efficiency, both on the job and during installation.

Our creative work plan recommended positioning Hancor as a leading manufacturer of storm water drainage products and systems for state, municipal, and residential construction applications. It should also leverage both Hancor's heritage and its commitment to new product technology and innovations, resulting in superior solutions for storm water management.

Multiple advertising targets were designated, including engineers and contractors involved in state and municipal storm water drainage projects as well as residential applications, and distributors.

Our proposed communications program included a series of full-page ads with an appropriate schedule of industry publications, as well as both employee and corporate brochures. While we were preparing these various materials, we made sure to make contact periodically with the employees, giving them input as to our progress and keeping communications lines open.

We also helped Hancor plan and produce their annual national sales and managers meeting in February 1995. It kicked off the new corporate brand, unveiling all the supporting materials to the employees: the new advertising, logo, corporate brochure, and employees brochure, among other elements. The tagline "Technology. Innovation. Solutions." was displayed on a large banner, while the meeting featured the theme of "the magic of turning vision into reality."

Importantly, Hancor also held workshops exploring strategies and tactics for sales to deliver the message of the brand to the marketplace and for managers to reinforce the branding concept with the employees.

When the national meeting concluded, each of the plant managers present received an edited videotape of the session. These were then shown to employees back at their home facility. Everyone had an opportunity to view it and to learn his or her own important role in the corporate branding program. Employees were also given a variety of special tie-in giveaway items, reinforcing once again the concept of Hancor's new corporate branding message.

ENSURING SUCCESS

To make "the magic" really work, of course, takes a good deal more than a new logo or tag line or brochure. The real magic begins and ends with the corporate brand and with how well the company uses it. By this I mean the entire company, management and employees, all of them, from the top down and the bottom up.

Does each and every one of them understand and support the corporate branding message? Do they utilize the corporate brand in every possible business communication? Does your corporate brand tell your various audiences exactly who your company is and what it and its products represent?

Hancor's people know what Hancor is and stands for. And they are working hard to promote that message of success via their corporate brand. It's starting to pay off.

OTHER WAYS TO REFLECT CORPORATE BRAND

"If nature has made any one thing less susceptible than all others of exclusive property, it is the action of the thinking power called an idea, which an individual may exclusively possess as long as he keeps it to himself; but the moment it is divulged, it forces itself into the possession of every one, and the receiver cannot dispossess himself of it."

—THOMAS JEFFERSON

As I stated at the beginning, this book is about an idea, a concept increasingly essential to business success. The idea is, of course, corporate branding. In discussing this concept, we have examined the use of many ideas by various companies in their efforts to create, promote, and maintain their corporate brands. A good number of these efforts focused on corporate advertising, integrated with brand advertising and other forms of company communications.

But a number of corporations promote their corporate brands without benefit of corporate advertising, and in some cases without benefit of any advertising. This section reviews several of the more unusual methods some companies employ to create and promote their particular corporate brands.

Like Attending a Protest Rally

Body Shop International is a chain of cosmetic stores. Well known for supporting controversial causes, Body Shop caters to customers who, to large extent, consider themselves socially conscious, who may even have been "activists" back in the '60s. Body Shop understands that it is possible for point-of-sale politics to distinguish a company just as readily and effectively as a slogan or logo.

Stuart Elliott writes in the *New York Times,* "Stepping into a Body Shop can be like attending a protest rally. Product labels plead against testing cosmetics on animals. Signs at the cash register promote recycling and conservation. Bags ask shoppers to join Amnesty International. Volunteers offer voter registration on the spot."[1]

Point-of-sale politics instead of point-of-sale hard sell may be a little different and perhaps not every company's cup of tea, but it seems to work well for Body Shop International. It creates and furthers a corporate brand most suitable for their targeted audience.

This New World Is "The Real Thing"!

In August 1990, the Coca-Cola Company opened its fabulous new "The World of Coca-Cola." This is a $15 million, three-story pavilion packed with state-of-the-art technological displays, unique interactive exhibits, and more than 1,000 pieces of Coca-Cola memorabilia.

"For years," says Company archivist, Philip F. Mooney, "we received calls from thousands of people from around the world who wanted to see something that didn't exist. Now it does. Finally there is one single place where fans of Coca-Cola can go to satisfy their thirst for everything associated with the world's most popular soft drink." At the time of opening, Roberto C. Goizueta, chairman and CEO, was quoted: "For business students, it will be a compendium of American marketing over the last 100 years. For Americans, it will be a demonstration of how Coca-Cola has helped shape and reflect their culture. For international visitors it will illustrate the Company's commitment to the global marketplace. For collectors of Coca-Cola memorabilia, it will be the ultimate destination. And for children it will be an enjoyable, educational experience."[2]

Pavilion director Marc Grauer noted that the pavilion is much more than a museum. "It's a showcase for the Company and its global reach," he said. "Every person who comes through this building is a consumer."[3] And to date more than 5 million consumers have visited The World of Coca-Cola since its opening in August 1990.

EXHIBIT C–1   WORLD OF COCA-COLA VISITOR'S GUIDE

The World of Coca-Cola is an entertainment and educational marvel for consumers, businessmen, and collectors fascinated with the rich heritage of the worldwide Coca-Cola system. The pavilion contains the world's largest assemblage of Coca-Cola memorabilia—more than 1,000 artifacts, presented in chronological order plus numerous interactive displays, high-tech exhibits, and video presentations. Visitors are taken on an exciting journey through the more than 100 years history of the world's most famous consumer product.

They especially enjoy, among other popular exhibits, the "Barnes Soda Fountain," a working replica of a 1930s soda fountain, named after an actual Georgia drug store. It features one of the first 1935 one-step fountain dispensers as well as an authentic 1940 jukebox that plays 20 recordings of original sheet music containing Coca-Cola in the lyrics or titles. Among the selections are "We Found That He'd Been Drinking Coca-Cola," and "The Coca-Cola Girl."

A 4,500 square foot retail store features the largest selection of Coca-Cola merchandise available anywhere. It offers visitors the latest in Coca-Cola trademarked clothing, collectibles, and contemporary and nostalgic gifts.

The World of Coca-Cola is but one segment of Coca-Cola's efforts at corporate branding. Many corporate involvements, such as the Special Olympics and World Cup soccer, and a totally integrated marketing communications program make the Coca-Cola logo the most recognized in the world today. But the pavilion is a unique and highly visible and effective aspect of their corporate brand.

Says Marc Grauer, "We are creating a fun and enjoyable place to visit, and we hope all our guests will leave with a good feeling about The World of Coca-Cola."

THE AD OR THE VODKA?

Here's a product whose very package shape becomes the ad: Absolut Vodka. Most people would be hard-pressed to distinguish one vodka from another, but Absolut's innovative advertising has made it an astounding success.

Depicted as just about anything from a Christmas tree to an aerial view of Central Park, a skyscraper to a ski slope, the Absolut package is featured in a different way in every ad. These employ a broad spectrum of timely icons to broadcast and reinforce Absolut's brand awareness.

As an added plus, Absolut ads go an unusual step further toward promoting the brand. Inspired by their variety and uniqueness, collectors now put them in albums and trade them with friends, much as they do baseball cards or stamps. How far this

EXHIBIT C–2   ADS FEATURING THE ABSOLUT PACKAGE IN A VARIETY OF TIMELY ICONS HAVE BECOME COLLECTIBLES

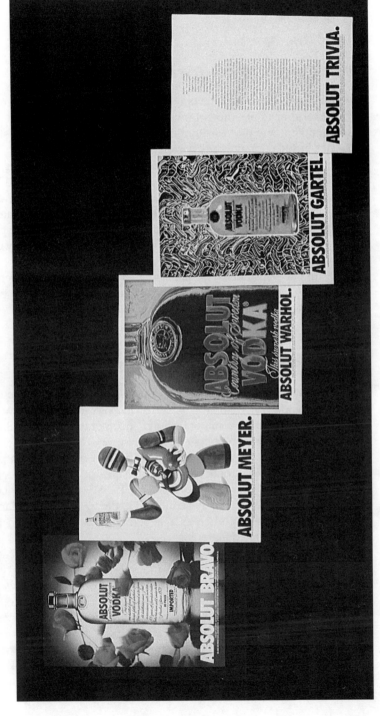

craze may spread is anybody's guess, but some people even collect Absolut ads today.

ONLY EVIDENCE OF TOTAL MARKETING

Absolut Vodka hasn't the only packaging today that is, in effect, the ad. For example, note DowBrands' Scrubbing Bubbles, Clearly Canadian, and the "Uh-Huh" on the Pepsi can"—marketing strategies based upon package design from the outset.

Consider packaging design as a pre-eminent marketing tool. The perfume industry, for example, has recognized this for a long, long time. Packaging is the only tangible and visible evidence of the total marketing effort. Packaging has a life longer than any marketing campaign, and is the only marketing vehicle seen more often, by more consumers, before, during, and after a sale than any other corporate sales effort.

In many instances, the package is the product and as such can play an unequalled part in building and promoting both brand equity and corporate brand.

REWARDS OF INCENTIVE MANAGEMENT

The following interview with Richard Sabo, assistant to the CEO, Lincoln Electric Company, Cleveland, Ohio, describes how one company's brand communications incorporates successfully an incentive management system.

"We are the world's leading manufacturer of arc welding products, and a major producer of industrial electric motors and cutting products. Not only are we concerned that our products be in demand, but also that they be utilized in the most efficient manner. Therefore a great portion of our communications program is in training and related materials.

"In addition to extensive employee and distributor education, we also train our customers to be knowledgeable in the use of our products to reduce their own production costs. Naturally, we are deeply involved in technical training on the community college, technical school, and high school levels. We want young people to come into our industry and be loyal to our product.

"As an adjunct to training, publishing is another area of our communications program. We put out a fine line of textbooks—34 titles in all. One, called *Procedure of Arc Welding*, has already sold over a million copies.

"Our entire communications program is carefully designed to establish a corporate image of a company that is not only very strong and very concerned with quality, but also very dedicated to its employees. Our business reputation is of a company that retains and conserves its work force because we have high confidence in our people. They know their jobs and do them extremely well.

"Communication is always encouraged. We like to promote an open mind policy and want our employees to feel comfortable in coming directly to management to resolve concerns. We also look to them for cost reduction suggestions. Last year we adopted nearly 500 of these for a savings of almost half a million dollars.

"Our communications program includes seminars on incentive management, the management style for which the company has become quite famous—a style of management that has actually become an integral part of our corporate brand.

Primarily, incentive management is a pay for performance program which gives each employee immediate insight as to his or her performance and pays on the basis of the number of quality pieces each produces.

"We find this management by commitment far more effective than management by control. In effect, we tell our employees that if they have the right attitude and are willing to work unlimited overtime, accepting job transfer in bad times, we will guarantee them 75 percent of the normal work week—30 hours of work but not a specific amount of pay or specific job function—however tough the economic times.

"We have had excellent results with this guaranteed pay for performance program, and there is a great demand by other companies for information on the system. Little wonder. It has been successful for us for more than 75 years, and is thoroughly bound up in our highly effective corporate branding program."

As these samples show, there are many ways to establish and promote a corporate brand. No one way is necessarily correct. At the Body Shop, point-of-purchase politics. For Coca-Cola, among other things, a whole new world in a magnificent pavilion/museum. Absolut's clever, collectible advertising, based on its package. The packaging itself for a number of other companies. And the impressive, all-encompassing educational and employee programs at Lincoln Electric. All different. All successful ideas for leveraging the corporate brand.

What is your special approach to corporate branding?

NOTES

1. Stuart Elliott, "When Products Are Tied To Causes," *New York Times,* April 18, 1992.
2. "A New World Opens," *Journey,* the magazine of the Coca-Cola Company, September, 1990.
3. Ibid.

INDEX